MW01503508

Black Violin, LLC
www.PashaSabouri.com
hello@pashasabouri.com

Ordering Information:
Quantity sales: Special discounts are available on quantity purchases.
For details, contact the publisher at the address above.

Design and Composition by Chad Peevy

Printed in the United States of America

First Printing, 2017 :: First Paperback Printing, 2020

ISBN 9798685386175

First Edition

I'd like to dedicate this book to all of the wonderful supportive people who have constantly encouraged me to reach for the stars. From my amazing private studio and mentors to my wonderful family and ever supportive husband. Thank you for teaching me to make my dreams a reality and to always be learning - when we stop learning, we stop growing.

UPBEAT

A Guide to High School, Business and Life for Young String Musicians

contents

A NOTE FROM THE AUTHOR

This book has been formulating in my mind for a long time. The advice you'll find here derives from the simple idea that musicians – even young musicians – ought to be equipped for the business side of their careers. Without that preparation, the most talented musicians can fail to make a living.

As you read, you'll encounter the same recommendations that I give my college bound music students and their parents. The information in these pages has led many of them to get into good colleges and pursue remarkable careers. If you take it to heart, it can do the same for you.

To all the parents out there, thank you for reading Upbeat. Thank you also for the interest you've taken in your child's passion. The world needs more parents like you! That said, the advice within these pages is intended for students. Read it if you like, but then share this book with your child and encourage them to digest it independently. This book was written to prepare them for their future career, and that's something they'll need to do on their own.

Finally, a quick word about the title.

In music, an "upbeat" is the last beat in a bar that precedes the downbeat. It marks a transition, and is characterized by the anticipation of the next movement of music. In life, "upbeat" refers to a positive and optimistic mood.

I hope this book can be both.

Enjoy,

Pasha Sabouri

Dr. Pasha Sabouri

> "I'VE NEVER KNOWN A MUSICIAN WHO REGRETTED BEING ONE. WHATEVER DECEPTIONS LIFE MAY HAVE IN STORE FOR YOU, MUSIC ITSELF IS NOT GOING TO LET YOU DOWN."
>
> – VIRGIL THOMSON

Being a musician is wonderful. There are challenges and there are stresses, but I wouldn't change it for anything. It's been the defining decision of my life, and I remember exactly when I made it.

Growing up, my parents always wanted me to play an instrument. I was a 12-year-old student attending Greenspun Middle School in Henderson, NV when I finally decided to give the piano a try. We weren't quite sure if the piano was in the category of orchestra or band, so I went into the orchestra room and asked the teacher if I could start playing piano in the orchestra.

She turned to me and said "Well, we don't have piano in orchestra but we do have these instruments." She showed me a violin, viola, cello, and a bass. At the time, I was very short – maybe around 4'3" – so I decided I was going to play the smallest instrument available.

I took the violin home, and realized quickly how much I enjoyed practicing and playing it. It wasn't practice that motivated me to play the violin for a career, though. That happened the first time I heard Itzhak Perlman on CD. (That's right: compact disc! We weren't lucky enough to have everything at our fingertips back then.)

The album was titled Bits and Pieces. In 12 years, I had never heard anything so beautiful and full of character. Every track was full of gems. I was enamored.

Bits and Pieces was so inspiring that I knew on my first listen that this was what I wanted to do for the rest of my life. So that's what I did.

Somehow, I doubt that my experience is totally unique. There are a million kids out there with memories just like mine, hoping to become professional musicians. You're probably one of them.

Yet many of them will end up as accountants, designers, teachers, or one of a thousand other things. Some will consider their decision to be a good one. Others will look back regretfully at the decision to change their course and wonder whether they could have pulled off a successful career in music.

I don't want you to wonder. I want you to know.

When I started taking violin lessons, I was already twelve years old. Most violinists begin before their sixth birthday, so I was already very far behind. By the time I graduated from high school, I had made significant strides but remained way less talented than the peers I would meet in college. Fortunately, dedication and a big work ethic helped me catch up. Today, I'm a music teacher, performer, author, and manager of my own festival. I make a satisfying living off my work, and I think you can too.

Whether you're a prodigy on the strings or a beginner playing catch-up like me, I want you to know that a career in music is absolutely within your reach. I can't pretend that each of you will play to sellout crowds or write this generation's masterpieces, but what I can promise is that our industry is big enough for all of us.

You just need to be willing to work.

I believe that most people can achieve nearly any goal. I truly do. The problem is that we tell young people that without ever saying how it's done.

That's what this book does. Instead of filling you with inspirational jibber jabber that makes you feel good but ultimately leaves you empty-handed, this book will show you what a real musician's life looks like and explain in clear detail how to position yourself for it. It's the tool I never had, and the one that will put you on the fast track to musical success.

In the first chapter, we'll look at life after high school and figure out whether you're a good fit for a music major in college. Then, we will explore the life of a normal musician, including all the career options that may be available to you. After that, we'll move onto chapter 3, "Preparing for Your Future While You're Still in High School." This is the longest and most important chapter in the whole book. In it, you'll find detailed instructions about how to become mentally and technically prepared for college. In the next three chapters, I'll explain your high school timeline, talk about the application process and teach you how to find the perfect college, university, or conservatory for you. Finally, there's chapter 7, one last chance for me to touch on the most important concepts and give a little advice.

CHAPTER 1

SHOULD COLLEGE BE YOUR NEXT STEP?

For the most talented and creative stars among us, a college education may not be necessary for success, but for us mere mortals college is the best way to develop your talent, network with other musicians, and lay the foundation for a career in classical music.

It's not perfect, though. Despite what you may imagine, a music major is not all about practicing and performing. At most colleges and universities, you will still need to complete a bunch of non-musical coursework, including stuff that's not totally relevant.

The "general education" requirements you'll find at most schools exist to get students of all majors to the point where they can handle their more difficult, major-specific work. Conservatories, on the other hand, are arts schools. Their curriculum includes much less general coursework than a typical two- or four-year school because their students are all on similar career tracks. *(We'll talk much more about the different types of schools in chapter 6, "Selecting Your School." Until then, I'll be referring to all types of post-high school education collectively as "college.")*

In the end, your basic coursework is determined by your specific school, but most colleges call for:

- Some basic English and composition
- A few math courses of your choosing
- A science lab
- A library studies class
- One or two physical education classes
- Public speaking

That last one stops lots of students in their tracks. "Public speaking? What do I need that for? I want to be an orchestral performer, not a motivational speaker!" Well, you're not alone. There are thousands of accounting, business, and American studies majors who are thinking the same exact thing. Colleges just happen to hold public speaking in high regard, so nearly everyone has to take it. What your non-musical peers don't know is that your class schedule has courses which would force them, crying and terrified, into a dark corner.

Sure, all those other students need to take public speaking, but music majors also need to take public performance classes.

Required Class: Singing

If your idea of a perfect vocal audience is a shower curtain, a few bottles of shampoo, and the reassuring flow of steamy water, then majoring in music is going to take some getting used to. That's because instrumentally-focused musicians like you and me rarely give much thought to music's vocal component. In college, that will change.

Nearly all music majors will frequently have to sing. Some will need to sing a lot. Depending on the musical emphasis you decide to pursue, some music programs will require you to take voice classes in all eight semesters of undergraduate study. You may not need that much vocal education, but every program will require singing as part of your music theory classes.

(More on those later!)

Vocal training is conducted in the classroom as well as in one-on-one settings. That means you will sometimes need to sing in front of a classroom full of your peers and other times you will need to sing in a quiet room in front of a single instructor.

I'll let you decide which is more frightening.

To all of you stuck in a cold, panicky sweat: relax. Although they take some getting used to, vocal training is really not so bad. You may not put on your best performance every time, but that's okay. No one in the room with you is perfect (even if they seem like it). Plus, the hollow feeling in your stomach isn't permanent. That nervousness eventually goes away. Practicing might not make you perfect, but even the most neurotic vocal students begin to feel comfortable after the first semester or so. I know that I did.

Learning how to sing *(or learning how to sing well)* benefits all musicians, even if you don't ever plan to be a vocal performer. That's because the voice is the most common instrument on earth. Utilizing it should be a goal for any music major. Learning how to sing well increases your appreciation of other musical arts, immerses you in music in new and challenging ways, and improves your understanding of pitch and range.

I've found that the best way to use my singing skills is to sing the "phrases" the way I would like to play them on my instrument. Because string instruments are supposed to imitate the human voice, nothing clarifies the sound quite like vocalizing it.

Required Class: Piano

As part of the core curriculum, many collegiate music programs also require their strings students to study the piano. If you already play the piano, way to go! This part of your musical education should be something you're very comfortable with. For those of you who do not play the piano, please, keep the groaning to a minimum.

This sort of "required instrument" policy may sound unfair for high school students who have only ever focused on a single instrument, but if you want a musical degree worth its salt, you're going to need some familiarity with a variety of instruments. In fact, you may have to study other instruments as well. It is not at all uncommon for a student to undertake vocal, strings, and piano performances in a single undergraduate career. In fact, if you pursue a music education major, you will take semester-long classes on a variety of band and orchestral instruments.

There are a few reasons why I think that required piano is good for music majors. First, it places another instrument within your reach. Anyone who enjoys music enough to study it in college should be thrilled about the idea of picking up a new instrument. Another benefit is that it helps you read music more successfully by introducing you to an additional clef. The mental benefits don't stop with sheet music either. By intensively studying another instrument, you are frequently tested on your ability to identify pitch and clarify rhythms. A third mental perk is that piano skills help you make sense of all the chord analysis you'll see in theory class. Finally, piano strengthens your coordination. As a violinist, I received notable benefits from studying piano because it improved my ability to use both hands independently. Better coordination means I can play notes on my preferred instrument more reliably.

Most of us who have been through it agree that piano training is essential to the spirit of a music major, especially one who wants to study performance. Classical music is much broader than your primary strings instrument. You cannot begin to truly understand it until you've developed at least a moderately large skill set.

A few more benefits

In addition to establishing new skills and knowledge, exposure to the piano *(and other instruments)* has lots of other benefits.

It boosts imagination

Even if you only ever plan on playing a single instrument professionally, fiddling with secondary or hobby instruments engages your musical brain. The thought that it takes to express your musicality on a less familiar instrument can shake out all kinds of good ideas that you can apply to your primary instrument.

This type of "big picture" creativity is especially valuable if you ever wish to compose original music.

It allows you to be more collaborative

I won't ramble on about this too long, but one of the things that makes music so great is that it brings people together. Even in the world of popular music, you often find artists who seem entirely different coming together to record a single. That's because music is naturally collaborative. Musicians want to work together.

That can sometimes be a problem for specialists. Of course, if you're very talented and have a little name recognition, then your reputation alone may attract offers to collaborate on projects. If you only have one skill and no reputation, then it's much harder for you to join in on the fun.

And trust me, you want to join in on the fun.

It allows you to compose more broadly

Right now, you probably have it in your head that you want to be a performer and not a composer. That's pretty normal. Most teenage musicians that I meet enjoy playing their instrument so much that they cannot imagine any other type of music career.

Down the road, however, you may find yourself interested not just in performing a particular piece of music, but creating it yourself. If you're only comfortable with your primary instrument, you'll likely be limited as to what you can create, and you're way too young to start shutting the door on possible career choices already.

It's a good thing

Piano classes are a great example of why college is such a good choice for young people who want musical professions. Piano stretches your mind, builds new skills, and opens new doors.

Getting Deep in Music History

Although most don't count it among their favorite courses, every student will benefit from expanding their knowledge of music history. As rich as many compositions are, their depth is truly revealed by the context in which they were written.

The way I see it, every composer has a unique language that is expressed in their music. Just like any other language, there are a variety of ways to use it. Mastering the performance of a single piece is like studying French – but only to have one, very specific conversation. At the end, you may be able to purchase a few baguettes from a street vendor, but you don't know French. In order to really get a full comprehension, you need to go deeper.

That's what music history does.

Music history provides a fascinating backdrop to the music you love and fully enriches it, so that you can enjoy it even more.

One of my favorite examples of how music history improves a listening experience comes when listening to Dmitri Shostakovich's String Quartet Number 8. It is a sad, fearful, and threatening piece "whose moods throughout its five movements reflect various shades of black." [1]

Listen to the piece in isolation and you cannot help but admire it. Listen to it in context and you'll fall in love.

A few people debate it, but most agree that the entirety of the piece is a tribute to the opposition of fascism. After all, the dedication reads, "In Remembrance of the Victims of Fascism and War." The evidence for this interpretation is emphasized at the beginning of the fourth movement, "when three notes are repeated against a low drone: the sound of anti-

1http://www.quartets.de/compositions/ssq08.html

aircraft flak and the menacing whine of a bomber high in the sky above."

Shostakovich wrote String Quartet Number 8 in a feverish three-day period shortly after visiting the bombed-out ruins of Dresden during World War II. That experience explains why he may have been motivated to incorporate the sounds of battle into his composition.

What stands out above all is that the composition is remarkably sad. It seems to capture the right mood, though, if Lev Lebedinsky is to be believed. A friend of Shostakovich's, Lebedinsky has claimed that the composer wrote String Quartet Number 8 as the epitaph to his life, and planned to commit suicide shortly after completion.

The personal and historical contexts of the composition enrich the music, revealing the artist's feelings and motives. This is why the importance of music history cannot be overstated, especially for current and future composers. When you know the historical composers, important dates, stylistic periods, and the historical or personal influences guiding a composition, the details become apparent. The patterns make sense. The music comes alive.

Theory, Theory, and More Theory

The last potential deterrent for many would-be music majors is all the music theory that is required.

As a music major, you don't simply learn how to make your instruments produce beautiful sounds, you also need to know how to identify, describe, notate, and utilize those sounds. And you need to do it at a high level. In college, it will not be enough to read sheet music and play the proper notes anymore. You will also have to demonstrate excellence in a number of skills, such as:

- Identifying notes by ear, including whether they are sharp or flat
- Recognizing pitch
- Naming and playing on a variety of scales
- Understanding interval relationships of notes and how to use them

effectively
- Implementing a variety of chords
- Comprehending keys and key structures
- Voicing across different instruments (like in hocketing)
- Speaking, writing, and reading about these things in an informed way

Depending on your level of training before you reach college, you may find the theory aspect of your studies to be fairly familiar. Or you may find it to be an entirely new challenge altogether. Either way, the theory is an important component of your musical studies and one you'll need to spend a lot of time attending to.

Still Feeling Confident?

If one of those four areas – singing, piano, history, or theory – are worrying you a little bit, that's okay. Don't let it scare you away from your passion. College is a time for challenging yourself and learning new things. Any music program that didn't force you out of your comfort zone at least a little bit wouldn't be worth the paper that your degree was printed on. You need to try new and difficult things if you want to grow.

It can be tough, but I know that you can handle it! You just need to put in the work.

One other thing

I know that you want my honest opinion, because you're really serious about your college and professional careers. That's why I have to tell you one more thing:

You will not be taught all the skills you will truly need for a successful music career after graduation.

That's because the institutions that guide musicians are incomplete. They teach you how to use your instruments, but never your wallet, head, or heart. The biggest offenders are the educational institutions. I'm talking about colleges, universities, and conservatories.

Despite their incredible, obvious, and practical value, most schools just don't teach the real-world skills you need. I've even known a few high-minded musical types who considered these vital talents "beneath" them *(for reasons I've never understood)*.

Their absence from the curriculum of America's music schools is perhaps the most egregious failure of the academic music world. As far as I'm concerned, it is unjustifiable. What are they, you ask? What are these holy-grail talents that will take your musical ability and jumpstart your career by five years or more? That's easy. They're business skills.

The Mistake Colleges Make

There is no doubt that academia lets down its music students. All of the instrumental and theoretical components are there, but most of the practical lessons simply go untaught. I'm talking about lessons that teach students how to network and build relationships, find work and handle finances. Once you've reached the point where your musical talent is worthy of a paycheck, these business skills tend to be the difference between success and failure.

And for some reason, they are rarely taught – but why?

The reason that valuable, career-making skills aren't taught in music-specific business classes is that everyone seems to misunderstand the transition from student to graduate. There is this idea floating around that someone who graduates with a college degree has everything they need to succeed.

But it's just not true!

When you're creating, teaching, and performing at a professional level, music is a job. It's not a final exam or a book report. It requires a professional attitude, attention to detail, ongoing commitment, business sense, and the knowledge and understanding that college offers. If you don't have it all, you don't have a career.

What makes things even worse is that finding a good entry-level music career is harder than ever. We can't get through school and rely on a single employer to carry us along. Employment just doesn't work like that anymore. Our grandparents could work with the same company for 30 or 40 years, support their families comfortably, and then retire with a lifelong pension. You're unlikely to have that experience. Nowadays, there are no retirement guarantees. Employees are left to fend for themselves.

This is even truer for music majors because a long music career almost never involves a single employer. Most of the musicians I know are entrepreneurs. They're out there performing for a different client every week - writing, producing, teaching, you name it. They didn't step into someone else's existing company structure. They had to build it for themselves, and you likely will too. You need to recognize that a profitable, lifelong career may not be waiting in the wings. You're responsible for your own success. You're a business owner and your product is you.

That's how you need to think. In fact, it's the first lesson of this book: music isn't just something you do; it's your business.

The Effects after Graduation

We all know that music is about more than money, but when it comes to your business, the money is definitely important. If you make poor business decisions, it's not just your music that suffers. You could drown in debt, miss your rent or mortgage payments, lose your car, and be condemned to a diet of tap water and bad frozen pizza. Proper business sense can make or break your future.

Whether you're operating a traditional company with hired employees or you're working solo, entrepreneurs are responsible for all the financial, managerial, and daily operating decisions. It's a lot harder than just showing up.

I'm not the only one who knows this either. Colleges know what awaits you, too. Still, they inexcusably continue to prepare you for only one type of career. *(We'll discuss the many career choices that you really have in the next chapter.)*

For us, the people least likely to have lifetime employers, the limited skill set offered in college can be debilitating. Until the academic perspective on this issue changes, musicians will have to find their own ways to learn about practical, real-world business matters. Lucky for you, you found a resource that is prepared to help you do just that!

The title of this chapter asks, "Should college be your next step?" So far, I've had a foot in each camp, giving you reasons why you should and why you shouldn't consider further education. Well, before you withdraw your applications and decide to go it alone, let me answer the question definitively: you should absolutely go to college.

The benefits of going to college far outweigh the drawbacks, even if they are big ones.

College Will Let You Down. Go Anyway.

The current system is not perfect. Colleges and universities have a long way to go before they strike a balance between academic and practical knowledge. Even with the shortcomings, though, I cannot recommend a music degree highly enough.

A career in classical music often begins with an education in classical music. An education isn't required if you're simply interested in a paying gig here and there *(I wouldn't recommend a full-blown college degree for a hobbyist)*, however if you want a true career in music, then you must get a musical education.

The structure and intimacy of a school's music program offers guidance and support as you discover the strengths and preferences you will utilize the rest of your career. The credibility of a recognized institution, and of its instructors, also validates your skills and gives you credibility too. The value of those benefits is hard to measure.

Plus, college is an opportunity to improve technical skill, establish connections, and explore prospective career choices through discussion and internship. Once I've taught you how to get the most out of those situations, they will benefit you even more.

These days, there is even a strong cultural argument to be made for going to college. You see, complexity in lots of other industries has demanded the specialization of employees. As a result, would-be hires must demonstrate their expertise by earning a degree. This makes sense for lawyers, doctors, and other professionals who need technical knowledge to do their jobs. Unfortunately, that mindset has reached into nearly every corner of the American psyche, so that even the most amazing musicians must often present a degree or have their knowledge, skills, and commitment questioned.

Although it is probably a mistake to judge someone's talent solely on whether they went to college, it remains true that the foundation of most professional musicians' careers is their musical education, and I strongly recommend that you get one yourself. Just realize that it won't cover everything that a musician truly needs.

Your First Business Decision!

If music is your business, then college is your grand opening. You need to determine where to host it, how long it will last, and the size of the investment you're willing to make. That makes going to college your first business decision.

We'll talk about the major considerations for selecting a school in the final chapter of this book, but - for now - just know that business thinking will guide all of your decisions from this point forward.

CHAPTER 2

EVERYDAY MUSICIANS AND THE CAREERS THAT DRIVE THEM

In the first half of this chapter, I want to accomplish two incredibly important things. First, I want to dismiss the myth of the musical genius and explain why you don't need to have the natural abilities of Amadeus Mozart in order to have a long and prosperous career. Then, I want to talk about that future career and discuss what kind of options there are out there for people who don't end up as a solo, chamber, or orchestral performer.

Destroying the Myth

It is common for performers like you and me to experience doubt. No matter how many hours we practice or how convincingly we can play our favorite piece of music, there always seems to be this little voice reminding us of our greatest fears. You know what they sound like:

"You're going to mess up."

"Nobody believes you deserve first chair."

"Everyone knows you're not good enough to do this for a living."

People in all walks of life, from the most common to the most fantastic, frequently experience this same type of doubt. Spend a few minutes searching the internet and you can find some of the most famous and beloved celebrities discussing their own experiences with crippling cases of low self-esteem.

Will Smith, who has been successful in nearly every endeavor he's ever embarked upon, once admitted, "I still doubt myself every single day. What people believe is my self-confidence is actually my reaction to fear." [1]

In the 1970s, David Bowie established himself as a legendary pop star and cultural icon. He was able to sell countless records and fill stadiums with adoring fans. Still, he often struggled with doubt, admitting that he "had enormous self-image problems and very low self-esteem, which [he] hid behind obsessive writing and performing." Even in the face of screaming fans who believed he could do no wrong, Bowie felt inadequate. [2]

As far as I can tell, though, it is award-winning author Maya Angelou who best describes the feeling. "I have written eleven books," she explains, "but each time I think, 'Uh oh, they're going to find out now. I've run a game on everybody and they're going to find me out.'" [3]

Perhaps this feeling of inadequacy is stronger for celebrities and performers because they are constantly being critiqued, judged, and evaluated in a public way. I don't know.

What I do know is that the most devastating piece of self-doubt that the young people I teach experience is that they don't truly think they can make a living playing their instrument.

This is called the imposter syndrome. It describes the fear that you're simply not good enough and it cripples people who let it take over.

I know a little about imposter syndrome because I suffer from it personally. You think this book was easy to write? I needed the support of my husband, my friends, my students and my student's parents to convince me that my advice was good enough to go into print. "Isn't it a

1 http://highability.org/435/gifted-and-talented-but-with-insecurity-and-low-self-esteem/
2 http://www.huffingtonpost.com/anneli-rufus/5-superstars-with-low-sel_b_4775028.html
3 http://highability.org/435/gifted-and-talented-but-with-insecurity-and-low-self-esteem/

little egotistical," I'd ask them. "Who am I to write a book?"

Fortunately, I had enough people reaffirming my abilities that I began to buy in to what they were saying...most of the time. When I'm alone, I sometimes still feel like I'm not worthy of the work I'm doing. The imposter syndrome is insidious.

The Causes of Imposter Syndrome

Not everyone suffers from this eternal lack of confidence, but for those who do, it often never leaves. Because they feel like an imposter, there is a voice shouting in their subconscious every time they play in front of someone for the first time. It's there, whispering from the darkness behind the curtain before they take the stage. It's always, always there.

For the professional, this fear is no less common. In fact, professionals probably suffer from it more. Their concerns just take an advanced form. "I'm not good enough to ask for this much money." "This audience really knows music – they'll see right through me."

Although self-doubt is a problem for all humans, and not just musicians, I really do think that it weighs heavier on our minds than it does for other people. One reason why is that classical music is undervalued in America, causing clients to question our worth. Because our industry places such value on age, young professionals are particularly prone to suffering from imposter syndrome. They're terrified of hearing the awful question: who does she think she is?

Another reason why we are susceptible to imposter syndrome is that we frequently have direct interaction with the giants in our field. If you're the owner of a tech business, you might hear great things about a guy like Bill Gates, but you never get to meet him. Our world is different. We get to read and play the famous pieces of great composers. Sometimes we even get to play for famous musicians. With that kind of access, it's hard not to measure yourself against the best of the best.

The last reason that musicians suffer from doubt is that terrible myth.

You know the one. It permeates pop culture and has tricked us all at least once. It's the myth that musical success requires artistic genius, some innate natural ability that is just fighting to get out. In reality, genius is as rare as you think it is. You may need it to become one of the legends whose name never dies, but you do not need it to find success. I promise.

Still, the genius myth is worrisome. Of the three reasons that musicians are so likely to suffer from doubt - being undervalued, access to greatness, and the genius myth - it's the third that is the scariest.

The Nightmare Situation

I'm reminded of the scene from the film Good Will Hunting, where Will submits a mathematical proof to his wannabe mentor, Professor Gerald Lambeau. In the movie, Will is an intellectual powerhouse that Lambeau describes as a "once in a generation mind." His abilities are so advanced, that when he submits his work to Lambeau, the professor doesn't believe it is correct.

In the debate that follows, Will angrily lights the proof on fire. Realizing that something valuable is disappearing before his eyes, Lambeau flings himself onto the floor and beats out the fire with his sleeve.

Crumpled up on the floor of his own office, he complains to Will that "there's just a handful of people in the world who can tell the difference between you and me. But I'm one of them."

In that moment, Lambeau is forced to confront in-the-flesh genius. What does that feel like? He tells us, saying, "Most days I wish I never met you, because then I could sleep at night. And that I could walk around without the knowledge that there was someone like you out there."

Even for this world-renowned MIT professor and winner of math's highest award, the idea that he just wasn't good enough caused serious problems.

You may not be too interested in math, but I'm sure you can imagine how awful it must be to come face to face with the person who embodies all your self-doubt. This feeling is depicted beautifully in a scene from another film, Amadeus. In it, Antonio Salieri encounters Amadeus Mozart in the king's practice chamber. To give you an idea about how good Salieri was, consider this: he was such a skilled composer and competent instrumentalist, that he was the man teaching the king to play piano. Not too shabby.

He was among the most talented and successful music men of his day. There was no reason in the world for him to feel dissatisfied with his position.

Well, if you've seen the film *(or the play)*, then you know what happens next. When the king concludes his playing, a conversation ensues and Mozart plays Salieri's own piece back to him.

He plays it without sheet music, entirely from memory, and after only a single hearing, despite the fact that the king's performance was quite poor.

What's even more impressive is that while playing he carries on conversation and makes perfect, improvisational improvements to the original.

For everyone in the room, this demonstration is further evidence of Mozart's prodigy, which had been well-established since his childhood. For Salieri, it was every musician's worst nightmare come true. He had been compared to true musical genius and fallen short.

Salieri goes on to explain that the worst part of it all was knowing that the corrections were better, far better, than the original, and that he could never become the composer that Mozart was. Salieri's compositions were good. Mozart's were miraculous.

Whether they have seen these movies or not, many young musicians know the feeling. They live in constant fear of someone else's genius.

I understand this fear. After all, if people like that are out there, with the genetic deck stacked in their favor, then what chance is there for a regular person like me? Well, I say that your chances are excellent. There are two reasons why.

The first is that the myth of the musical genius is largely overstated. You could work in the classical music field for your entire life and never even meet one of the über geniuses we all fantasize about.

The second reason is that talent isn't the only factor for success. This is so important. In college, I knew musicians that were far more talented than I was, but not all of them were able to develop a career. There were also decent musicians who fell short of professional caliber only to later "catch up" and find success. I can even remember one musician who played like an amateur. Today, even that person is a successful, award-winning musician.

I understand the fascination with genius *(after all, who wouldn't be captivated by a mind like Mozart's?)* but it's not a real concern because you can succeed without it. You'll never stop striving to play at that level, and - who knows - you may even get there, but I'll say it again so that it really sinks in: you can succeed without superstar talent.

When the Myth Disappears

What you should be concerned with is your own attitude. It's the only thing you can really control, and it will have a huge impact on your career.

Even if there were loads of geniuses running around all over the place, their success would be out of your control. Stop looking to them to fulfill your self-doubts. Quit spending all your time worrying about what other people are going to think, too. It's counterproductive. It distracts you from your work and saps your confidence.

While we're at it, let's tackle this other negative idea that's been going around. You know, the idea that you're not good enough to do this professionally.

You are absolutely capable of both beginning and maintaining a career in music. If you had to audition on this very day, you might not make the cut, but don't worry. Today isn't the finish line. In fact, if you're in middle or high school, then you're much closer to the beginning than the end.

With all that time available to you, there's almost no limit to your potential success. That's the best part! You're so young that, with hard work, you can reach the top even without natural talent! Genius isn't a prerequisite for success. In fact, most musicians don't have even a glimmer of it.

Most of the successful musicians I know from school weren't exceptionally talented. They were good, but it wasn't natural for them. They worked hard. They practiced smart. They talked and argued and thought endlessly about their music, and one day they picked up their instruments and their talent was worthy of payment. That can be your story, too.

Even though the "gifted" musicians were better than these hard workers I knew, the gifted musicians lacked other skills. They had the talent, but they were only equipped to work for somebody else. The problem is that there aren't so many of those jobs around. Some of the people I knew did manage to land traditional jobs and become successful. Others fumbled around at the beginning and never really got out of the gates. Knowing how to get started at the beginning can make all the difference in the world.

And that is why you need this book.

Thinking About Your Future

If you dream of becoming a professional performer, you're not alone. It is the rare musician who doesn't fantasize about performing their favorite compositions on stage in front of thousands. Even among violinists, I suspect there is a deep-seated desire to be a sort of classical rock star.

These daytime fantasies are what motivate thousands of musical students to pay for private lessons, practice late into the night, and attend well-respected schools with excellent music programs. In the end, what nearly all of us are truly hoping for is to become our instrument's Yo-Yo Ma.

But few ever will, and that's okay.

Things to Consider

Young musicians *(and even many old ones)* often have narrow views of what a music career truly is. At one end is the passionate "starving artist" type, playing hundreds of cheap gigs per year. At the other end is the iconic virtuoso playing in major theatres for big crowds of important people. While both of those scenarios do exist, they ignore the countless, hard-working people in the middle. They ignore the "everyday" musicians.

Not everybody even wants to be a performer. Skilled musicians like you can make a good living, enjoy their work, and keep the arts alive without ever performing professionally – and many do.

I can hear you now. "You want me to major in music and not perform? What's the point?"

The point is that earning a position in the prestigious performances that we're taught to respect so highly is hard. Really hard.

Practice and auditions occupy most of your free time and can require frequent, expensive travel and time away from work. Plus, you are continuously exposed to exhausting evaluation, the high expectations are very stressful, and – if you finally get the job – you're not left with many free evenings. As cool as the result is, that path is not for everybody.

And why would it be? Pursuing any talent at the highest levels takes sacrifice. It leaves little room for much else. If you think that dedicating your life to music in such a way is worth the sacrifices you'll need to make, then by all means do it. Just don't think it's your only option.

The Wide World of Music

What I want to do now is show you some other choices, including ones that can offer you high income, respect in the industry, and opportunities to use your other skills, while fulfilling other passions.

Another reason I want to show you some of the other options is that every music career forces you to deal with other people in the industry, and they won't all be performers. Understanding some of the other roles out there will give you a better grasp of what those people do and how things work in the big picture. And it is a big picture.

There's a rich and rewarding professional world full of people who enable you to enjoy the music you love. They are the glue that holds the classical music industry together, and most of them spend little to no time performing *(even if that's what they wanted to do when they started)*.

Few probably knew what they would end up doing when they were still in college. Young musicians often stumble into their long-term careers accidentally. They go in with one plan and end up pursuing another career because their original path becomes a dead end, another job more closely matches their skills and personality, or an alternate endeavor proves more profitable.

Lots of people, inside and outside of the musical world, switch careers at least once. There's absolutely nothing wrong with it. After all, we pursue music because it makes us happy. When it becomes obvious that your professional choices aren't making you happy, then pivoting into a new career is the smart thing to do for your personal life and for your business.

Of course, things are easier if you are working with a plan.

Start Thinking About a Plan

If you want to try to become a professional performer, I would never try to change your mind. Playing my instrument is still one of the most satisfying and enjoyable ways to spend my time. I understand why you would want to make a career out of it. Still, preparing yourself early with one or more backup plans can save you a lot of difficulty down the road in case you ever feel the desire to pursue new options.

But when is the right time to choose?

I know that anyone reading this book is serious about a career in music, but it's a mistake to pick one prematurely. If you're still in middle school, then today isn't the day to choose your future career. All I ask is that you begin thinking about it. If you are a high school student, on the other hand, you do want to start considering your options. By your junior or senior year of high school, you should know what you want to pursue. Selecting your major is your second significant business decision. It will set the heading for at least the next ten years of your professional life. You want to choose wisely.

If you really cannot decide, I recommend consulting with your parents, teachers, and private instructor. The sooner you can decide, the better prepared you'll be.

If you find yourself having trouble, here's a tip. When you get down to two possible careers that you like equally, it's normally a good idea to go with the one that best fits the talents you already have. That's because music majors are much different than other majors. With music, they want you to have the foundation set before you get to college, while other programs are comfortable teaching you the basics when you arrive.

In order to demonstrate how many career choices you really have, and to help you develop a plan for yourself, I'm going to give you a really great resource. It's my Killer Career List and it contains over 50 music careers that are a good fit for music majors. You'll find it in the appendix of this book. It doesn't list every single job that's out there, but it does have a wide variety that will open up your eyes a little bit.

I don't want to send you racing off to the back of the book this very second, though, so I'm going to offer detailed descriptions of six additional careers right here. I've chosen these six because they highlight different skill sets and interests, as well as the variety of paths that the industry has to offer us. I think there's enough here to whet your appetite, but you'll definitely want to check out the full list when you're done reading.

Six Totally Awesome Music Jobs You May Not Have Considered

Teacher (K-12)

Some people preparing for a career in music look down on grade school music teachers as musicians who couldn't cut it. I don't buy that.

Grade school teachers are the front lines of classical music in our schools. Without qualified, passionate, capable educators teaching American kids how to play and appreciate music, how will they ever learn?

School districts are always looking for qualified music teachers, so you don't really have to worry about looking for work. It's also a career that lets you move around without struggling to find a new gig.

Where you are does matter, though. School districts have varying degrees of commitment to their music programs, meaning that grade school music teachers can make a good living or have trouble finding two dimes to rub together. Either way, we need strong music teachers to keep classical music alive for our kids.

Generally, teachers can expect to make salaries in the low $20s or as high as $60k/year annually.

Pit Musician

There are lots of events that require live music. When you are a pit musician, you can be a part of those events and use your instrument to elevate the performance to a new level.

Primarily used in musicals, ballets, and operas, pit orchestras are often the lifeblood of any stage performances that use them. Although most modern pit orchestras contain only about 25 musicians at once, there were times when they were much larger. Wagner's operas employed up to 100 pit musicians at a time. (Here's to hoping those days return!)

Even if you're the type of person who wants on-stage time and the prestige that comes with it, working in a pit orchestra may be a good decision early in your career. It looks good on a resume and can be a stepping stone for future orchestral performers.

If you're fortunate enough to perform in a Broadway orchestral pit, you can earn up to $1,500 each week.

Licensing Administrator

As musicians, it is important for us to support each other. If the arts are going to succeed in any meaningful way, then the artists need to have their work protected. They also need to be compensated fairly when their pieces are used. This is where the licensing administrator comes in.

Licensing administrators manage the copyrights to one or more pieces of an artist's work.

When a client wants to use the artist's music for a project of their own, they need licensing. You oversee the licensing process. You authorize the client to use the music, negotiating the terms of usage and the licensing fees, as well.

These unsung heroes are vital to the behind-the-scenes music economy. Usually, licensing administrators work for a music publishing house and can earn $50,000 each year.

Sound Recordist

When you exclude the stage, nearly all performance occurs in studios. Regardless of where a performance occurs, however, sound recordists are responsible for capturing it.

Sound recordists use their expertise to maintain the integrity of a performance. Musicians put a lot of trust in their recordist to get things right. An inexperienced recordist can spoil the performance of even the most spectacular symphony orchestras in the world. That can cost an organization or record label tons of money in lost sales.

One of the coolest aspects of the job is that you get to work with all kinds of expensive, powerful recording equipment. Depending on the relationship you have with your employer, you may even get to do some recording of your own!

Loads of sound recordists work as freelancers, so how often you work and how much you make will depend on how strong your business skills are. Something in the range of $55,000 per year isn't unreasonable if you work hard.

Video Game Composer

As the technology continues to improve, video games are becoming more visually impressive all the time. Developers and customers alike are yearning for a completely immersive experience. That means music.

Platforms like Steam now allow for independent developers with unique vision and exciting ideas to compete with the big guys. That means opportunities for creativity, paving the way for games like Journey, whose orchestral soundtrack broke into the iTunes top 10 [4] and reached 116 on the Billboard sales chart! [5]

For some people, video game composition is the marriage of two beloved activities. If that sounds like you, then working as an independent video game composer could be right up your alley. When you work for big budget developers, you can earn up to $2000 for every minute of music you write.

Marketer

Music is an art. It is also a business, and businesses need marketing.

Some people think that marketing is just sleazy "hard sell" advertising. That's not true. Honestly, there's an almost unlimited variety of musical marketing that an informed professional could pursue.

Think about it this way: anything in the musical world that is sold can benefit from marketing. The sellers of tickets, instruments, lessons, albums, studio and stage time, recording equipment, spare parts, and a bunch of other things are always looking for new ways to convince buyers that their products are worthwhile. You can be the one that persuades them.

Write magazine ads for an instrument manufacturer. Design a

4 https://www.theguardian.com/technology/gamesblog/2012/may/28/video-game-soundtracks-concept-albums
5 http://www.gamasutra.com/view/pressreleases/179112/sumthing_else_music_works_releases_journeytrade_official game_soundtrack.php

fundraising flyer for your local music camp. Organize a campaign for your favorite music store. Do whatever works.

Because you're plugged into the world of music, you're probably better suited to address the nuanced concerns that potential customers would express. You understand their problems, too. That's the secret to great marketing.

Like lots of other jobs, marketers earn according to a number of factors. The best of the best can easily earn six figures or more. Plus, good marketers divert money back into the music world, which benefits all of us.

A Little Bonus

Don't forget! If you want to see the full list, read through to the end of the book or go there right now. It's got 50 plus great musical careers that music majors need to know about. Not sure which careers suits you best? Take this book and discuss the list with your parents, music instructors, and guidance counselors, as well as any other mentors you might have.

Looking Beyond the Title

As someone who hasn't even started college yet, you need to know that whatever path you choose isn't a life sentence. You can change your mind later. You might end up having one title, ten titles, or none at all. What you call your career isn't important. What's important is that you start thinking about various careers, considering which choices are best suited for your personality, and evaluating what skills or processes you would be most interested in using on a day-to-day basis.

Don't stress yourself out wondering what you're going to do for "the rest of your life." Many musicians never end up going down a single path. Instead, they have a "portfolio career" that contains lots of pursuits.

Portfolio Careers

Earlier in this book, I hinted at the idea that most musicians succeed based on skills other than raw talent. One of those skills is their ability to diversify.

When you begin, you probably won't have a reputation. That means you won't be able to command much money. It could take years to scrape together a livable wage in your preferred career. So, what do you do in the meantime?

You do something else! It's not at all uncommon for a professional musician to direct their own ensemble, perform as a collaborative artist, and teach private lessons to local students. When musicians work multiple jobs simultaneously in this way, it's called a portfolio career.

A portfolio career is a professional lifestyle with at least a few pieces. Instead of holding down a single job, a "portfolio musician" juggles several jobs. The variety allows them to expand their professional network, develop a reputation, and pursue their passion *(even if it's not paying very well yet)*. Most musicians start out with a portfolio career and some, like me, never give it up.

Life as a Musician

To be truly prepared for a music career, even a portfolio career, you need to start taking specific actions now. Many of them are entirely practical, and the next chapter is chock- full of suggestions about what exactly you ought to do *(and how to do it)*.

First, though, I want to make sure that you really, really understand what the musician's life looks like. If you were paying attention closely to the few jobs I just mentioned, then you will have noticed that several of them are freelance positions.

In case you don't already know, freelancers are workers who don't work for just one company in the way that a regular office worker does. They go around completing work for any number of clients until their problems are fixed. Small freelance jobs may take just a few hours. Others may be ongoing and last for years. In many ways freelancing is just like performing for a living. You depend on many people for your livelihood, and most of all you need to depend on yourself.

Whether you're performing or freelancing *(as most musicians do, at some point)*, things aren't always rosy. Both lifestyles are significantly different from the 9-5 lifestyle that Americans are used to, and they have certain drawbacks.

Here are five of the most unexpected and challenging aspects of a musician's life and how to prepare for them.

Working Off-Hours

Take a minute and think about a few of the last musical performances you attended. If you want to include something from musical theatre or the ballet, that's fine. Count those too.

Now, as you think about them, I want you to try and remember when the performances were held. Exact dates aren't so important as the general information. Was it daytime or nighttime? Were they held on weeknights or on the weekends? If they're anything like the performances that I normally attend, they weren't held in the afternoon on a Tuesday.

While hosting performances on nights and weekends is great for the audiences who are working 9-5, it's not as awesome for those who are putting on the show. And that's my point.

Whether you're hitting the stage as a performer, or helping to facilitate the performance from behind the scenes, it's important to recognize that most musical work happens outside of traditional working hours.

Most people work during the daytime. They save their nights and weekends for entertainment, and since that's what we're offering them, we need to put on our performances when they're available to come and enjoy them. It's as simple as that. Performances happen in the evenings, and when they don't, they're normally going down on the weekends.

This schedule is great if you want to get in to see the dentist, but it's terrible if you want to keep up with your favorite sports teams, go out to dinner with your friends, or see a performance yourself.

How to prepare: Buy a calendar or datebook and use it religiously. Because your schedule is going to be more erratic than it is in high school, it's a good idea to practice organizing yourself while things are still easy.

Inconsistent Pay

I have all kinds of friends with "normal" jobs. They show up for forty hours every week and a couple of times each month, the company cuts them a check.

Unless they're working commission-based positions, it doesn't matter whether they had five customers or five hundred. They're getting paid no matter what. That's money that they can use to buy groceries, pay the landscaper, or see a movie. Being able to count on a steady paycheck is the best thing about traditional employment, and it's something that most of us won't be able to do *(at least not early in our careers)*.

If you're out there working on your own as an independent contractor, you only get paid when you're working. There are no steady paychecks rolling in like there are with more reliable careers. A particularly slow month could come to an end before you collect enough money to make a utility payment or send off the rent check.

The good news is that a particularly successful month could earn you six months' wages in a single shot. Handling the "feast or famine" nature of self-employment is key to the future of any successful musician.

How to prepare: Open a savings account. We'll talk about the specifics of a budget later, but developing the habit of saving money now will really help you out down the road.

Taxes *(and other money problems)*

Benjamin Franklin said that the only things that were certain in life were death and taxes. He wasn't kidding.

When I was in high school, I worked a part-time job as a violinist at a Persian restaurant. Every week I took home a tiny little paycheck, made smaller by the taxes that were taken out of it. Back then, I used to hate that my taxes were taken out automatically. Nowadays, I wish it were that easy.

Unfortunately, when you work for yourself, there's no employer involved to ship off your tax payments for you. That's something you need to do for yourself. Another problem is that there's no one to help manage your health care benefits or your retirement fund either. These are among the many obstacles to successful self-employment as a musician.

It is important for you to understand how and why these financial matters work the way that they do. Even if you end up landing a job where you work for someone else, such as a film composer for an independent production studio, you will benefit from knowing where your money is going and the ways for you to control it.

How to prepare: Read a money book. Specifically, read a book about managing money.

Something like "The Money Book for the Young, Fabulous & Broke" by Suze Orman should do the trick.

Low Job Security

Whether you work independently or for an employer, your role is the same. You work hard, you get paid. Unfortunately, all the hard work in the world cannot build a strong client-contractor relationship. There is a bias among some *(though not all)* employers that leads them to a damaging conclusion: freelancers are disposable.

When you work for a company, you're "part of the family." Letting you go is considered a loss and everyone would prefer not to do it. Most independent contractors, on the other hand, are outsiders. They're coming in for a brief stint to do a little work, but it's not personal. It's business. If they do a poor job, cost too much, are suddenly unneeded, or ruffle feathers with their opinions, they can easily be fired without any real consequence.

This is true of freelance web designers, photographers, journalists, and – of course – musicians. As someone who works for themselves, you need to be aware of your role with clients. Even though your working relationships can *(and should)* be positive, you're still vulnerable.

Of course, the differences between you and traditional employees aren't all bad. If one client sets you free, you probably have a few more who will continue to send you checks. If your traditional counterpart gets let go by his employer, it's the only client he's got and the money will just stop rolling in.

How to prepare: Never stop working your contacts. Someone with a good reputation and strong relationships will never be out of work for long. As a student, this means maintaining strong friendships with your peers and open dialogues with your instructors.

Weak Structure

For millions of people, the time set on their alarm is picked very carefully. They wake up when they wake up because they know exactly how much time they need to get ready for their day. It's three minutes to brush their teeth, fifteen minutes in the shower, ten minutes to get dressed and grab a cup of coffee, then it's off to the office.

That tight schedule lasts all day long because their full-time office jobs provide them with such strong structure. They know when they're going to get up, get in the car, have a meeting, eat lunch, file some reports, struggle with traffic, and eat dinner. Their life works like clockwork because someone else is calling the shots.

Musicians who run their own business *(that's you!)* get to organize their schedules for themselves. If they want to, they can fly by the seat of their pants. Their entire calendar could be a Post-It note that reads "wing it."

You're probably thinking that this sounds wonderful. So did I. The lack of formal structure was one of the things I was most excited about when I realized I wasn't going to have a "boss."

But here's the thing. Although structure takes away some of our fun, it does have one incredible benefit: productivity. As a professional of any kind, you need to be productive. No one *(that is to say no one smart)* is going to pay you just for existing. It's absolutely vital that you are able to get work done even without the pressure of a parent, teacher, or supervisor checking in on you.

How to Prepare: Start a working routine. The power of routine is undeniable when it comes to getting stuff done. Block time for homework, studying, and practice, and do not deviate. Also, check out "The One Thing" by Gary Keller.

The Power of Practical Advice

Under each of the five drawbacks to performance and/or freelance careers in the music industry, I've included simple ways to prepare yourself. They are affordable, easy ways to build real skills.

Building a foundation in this way can save you hundreds of hours and thousands of dollars down the road. There's no doubt that you're going to need the skills I mention. The question is whether you develop them now, later, or not at all.

If you do begin developing them today, you'll enter college with a handful of intangible talents that few of your classmates will have. Transitioning into a career after graduation will be that much easier because you'll be equipped to handle the difficulties. If you don't develop the skills now, you'll make mistakes, fail to impress clients, and cost yourself lots and lots of money.

What sounds better to you?

I've mentioned several times already how important it is to go to school and get a strong music education, but so many of the skills you'll need for professional success aren't taught in a classroom.

You'll need to be organized, punctual, and professional. When we're talking about skills so easy to learn, why would you wait? You can get started today by implementing my advice right now:

1. Purchase and use a datebook or calendar for tracking your schedule.
2. Open a savings account and deposit money frequently.
3. Buy a financial book. *(As I write this, there are copies of "The Money Book for the Young, Fabulous & Broke" by Suze Orman online for less than $10!)*
4. Send an email to a different contact each week. Peers and teachers are fine for now.
5. Establish immovable homework, studying, and practice times. Do not deviate.

Follow these tips and you will already have business sense years ahead of your classmates.

Advice for Two Popular Career Choices

Although there are tons of great musical opportunities out there, most students imagine themselves doing one of two things: performing or teaching. You might have different plans for your future, but if you fall into one of those two categories, here is some advice.

Pursuing Performance

Do you want to be an orchestral, chamber, or solo musician? I understand the draw. As someone who's been in the industry for a while, I also understand the reasons why you might not want to pursue one of those careers.

Imagine you want to be a soloist. You can picture it now: live stage performances, studio album releases, interviews on NPR. Sounds great, right? But I wonder...

Will you be happy on the road for 200, or more, days each year? Are you comfortable with living out of a suitcase? Do you enjoy viewing amazing parts of the world from airports and hotel room windows? If you're fine with all of that, then congrats! You may have found your perfect career. But if that lifestyle sounds like something you would eventually come to resent, you should strongly consider doing something else.

Some people think that they want to go down a certain path, but realize later that they've overlooked obstacles they can't endure. If you can avoid that pitfall, you want to do it.

The trick is to recognize what is important to you. Every career has its perks and its disadvantages. Knowing what's really involved with the career that you pursue will help you figure out which perks bring you the most joy and which disadvantages cause the biggest headaches. Anytime you gain interest in a particular career, I recommend you write out all the things you believe you would love and hate about it. Take the list to your private teacher and discuss it with them. Their feedback will provide great insight into whether that career is in line with how you envision your life in a few years.

Advice for Future Educators

If Music Education is something that you're looking into as a possible career, then you need to be thinking about what you can do in your high school years to help you achieve that goal. Here are just a few ideas:

- Ask teachers to observe their lessons so that you can observe their teaching style
- Try administering a lesson while your teacher observes and critiques your style
- Take some courses on pedagogy *(that's the study of teaching methods and practices)*

These are just a few things that could help you decide if teaching is your true calling. They can also help you get some practical experience before you start your first semester at college.

To obtain a music education degree in college, you must spend multiple semesters learning other instruments. During the summer, it could be a good idea to try and learn how to play a little bit of a different instrument. *(I'm not saying you should sacrifice time on your main instrument to learn a different one. I'm simply recommending you take advantage of your lighter schedule.)* In college, you will learn another instrument while simultaneously taking all your core courses. Failing to meet your primary instrument goals won't be acceptable, no matter the reason. Get a head start this summer and you can avoid getting overwhelmed later.

Do You Have What It Takes?

Every successful musician I've ever known had skill, but few of them were truly impressive based on talent alone. You don't need to be genius to make a living in our business.

If you're reading this book, you're already demonstrating that you have some of the other skills you'll need. You're passionate about music, humble enough to recognize that you don't know everything, and committed enough to invest in your learning. Based on that information alone, I'd say that you are probably on the path to becoming a professional musician.

Just remember that there are lots of paths. If you want to be a performer, great! If you don't, that's great too! Sometimes you just need to find out what your strengths are and capitalize on them. The important thing to remember is that success rarely happens overnight. You're going to need to work.

You may need to work more than one job at a time. In fact, you probably will. That's all right. Working a portfolio career has served me well. I have lots of free time, make plenty of money, and get to enjoy music. It works for me because I work hard and I have the right attitude about my career.

I take things seriously, never forgetting that each of my income streams are part of one business.

If you do that, you'll be just fine.

In the next chapter, you'll find highly specific advice that will improve your business skills even further. There will also be advice about sharpening your technical skills. Better yet, it's advice that you can put into action right now!

CHAPTER 3

PREPARING FOR YOUR FUTURE WHILE YOU'RE STILL IN HIGH SCHOOL

Up until this point, I've described what college will look like, the path your career may take, and some of the skills you'll need for success. While all of these things are important for you to consider, they are all for the future. If you want to be a professional, you cannot just wait until Future You decides to move into high gear.

You need to start now.

Your 8 Keys to Future Success

This chapter is a goldmine of practical advice. If you follow the suggestions I lay out for you here, you'll be among the most prepared music students at your college. You'll still have the music side of things to address, but your frame of mind will be unmatched.

You're going to have to read the whole chapter, but here's a sneak peek at my top tips for college prep:

1. Start sight singing
2. Try your hand at piano
3. Take music classes
4. Study theory
5. Support musicians
6. Work all summer
7. Relearn practice
1. Get money-smart

These are things you can start doing right now to improve your skills and develop a professional outlook. I really want to make sure that you have what you need to get started, so I'm going to give you a useful tool or exercise with each key, just to put you on the right track.

Key #1: Learn Sight Singing

Some people hate the idea of singing in front of a group. Others love it. For me, it always feels like an adventure!

In the second chapter, I discussed how singing is an essential component of any music major's school career. Did that worry you? If so, let me ease your mind: I overstated things a bit.

You may have to do some singing, of course, but you will almost never be expected to become a performance level singer. My school didn't require me to take vocal lessons but I did have to sing in front of the class on a weekly basis.

Your experience won't necessarily be the same as mine, but if you're a string player, there's a pretty good chance that serious vocal classes are not in your future. Unless your career plans are taking you down the path of vocal performance, you'll probably be just fine learning primarily how to sing for pitch identification.

Tip for Key #1

Try this: Start every personal practice session by singing the piece you're about to play. Sing it exactly as you'd like to play it. When you begin to play, compare the sound your instrument makes to the sound your voice made.

What Exactly Is Sight Singing?

Sight singing is the ability to read musical notation and turn it into vocal music at first sight. It is not a performance art and it is the one type of singing that you will absolutely need to be familiar with if you're going to do well in school.

In many ways, sight singing is like reading English. Because you can speak English, you know what the words sound like. Whether you elect to read them silently or aloud, the words are creating sounds inside your mind. You can "hear" the author's words. In situations where you are very familiar with the writer, you can even hear their voice as you read.

That's how sight singing works. It creates an intimate connection between the way that notes are displayed on paper and the way they are heard when played aloud. This has a lot of value.

How To Learn Sight Singing

Fortunately, learning to sing on sight doesn't require much. You can do it with the help of a piano. All you need to do is play a note. After listening carefully, you should attempt to sing the same note, matching pitch.

If you cannot identify notes by ear, then you probably want to practice that first. There are countless resources online *(many of which are free)* that can help you learn that skill. Once you feel comfortable identifying notes, move on to repeating them. You can practice with a piano, by partnering up with a friend or instructor, or using software available online.

If you don't have access to a piano, you can also practice with an electronic tuner or even your own instrument. I don't recommend it as a preferred method, but it can work for you in a pinch.

Another thing I don't recommend is joining your school's choir just to obtain this skill. If you want a vocal career, then go ahead and get all the experience you want. Just don't think you must join just to learn sight singing.

Benefits Of Sight Singing

Ask any serious instrumentalist whether sight singing is important, and he or she will definitely say yes. Ask them why and they might struggle to come up with the right answer.

The way that I see it, becoming a proficient sight singer has four clear benefits.

Improved Sight Reading

Sight singing makes you better at sight reading because they are so similar. With sight singing, the sounds come out of your mouth. With sight reading, they come out of your instrument. Although each requires their sound with different muscles, the process of reading on sight is nearly identical to sight singing. Learning one improves the other.

Faster Mental Processing

The second benefit is speed. Just as with a computer, fast processing speed is important for a musician.

Sight singing happens in real-time. If you need to take a few minutes to review the material before the sounds start coming out, you're not doing it right. As you practice sight singing, your brain builds more efficient pathways between the input *(musical notation)* and the output *(the way music sounds)*. This enables you to absorb, process, and play music much more quickly. I don't think I need to explain why that's a good thing.

More Preparation Time

When you are sight reading during a performance, you need to remember what you've seen only briefly. Once it has passed through your eyes, into your brain, and down to your fingers, you can forget it. *(And most people do.)*

Though it only takes a moment, the ability to hold the information in your brain longer makes playing well easier. Sight singing improves that memory.

Skilled sight singers remember what they've seen longer than amateurs, allowing them to look further ahead and prepare for what is coming next. This short-term musical memory doesn't last more than a few seconds, but still provides the musician with precious processing time.

Precise Pitch Identification

Perhaps the most obvious benefit of sight singing is that it strengthens your ability to identify pitch. If you can identify pitch accurately, then you are more likely to produce it accurately.

Why Sight Singing Is Extra Important For String Players

Sight singing is valuable for all musicians, no matter their preferred instrument, but it is particularly important for string players. That is because strings imitate the human voice. Our job is to be "the voice" of all musical compositions without a vocal component.

Every piece of music that I play can be easily reproduced vocally. As a strings player, you should always be able to sing a phrase the way you want to play it. Personally, I sing my material all the time! Even when my violin is tucked away in its case and my mind is somewhere else, I'll find myself singing a piece I've been working on recently. It really helps to digest the music and get a fuller understanding of the way it feels and sounds.

"Playing" your music vocally can reveal useful details about a piece. Reproducing it without your instrument draws your attention to the way that specific notes are highlighted, how passages are connected, and the way the tone is conveyed to the listener. The best part is that you don't have to be a very good singer to receive these benefits. Regularly practicing sight singing will give you all the skills you need!

Key #2: Get Familiar with Piano

Unlike singing, piano plays a central role in your music education during college. In fact, most music majors are going to take two years of piano classes before they can graduate.

The good news is that you aren't required to have any experience ahead of time. You can show up to day one of your college career without ever having a piano lesson and still be right on track. Almost no one else will know what they are doing either!

But that doesn't mean piano isn't helpful.

Tip for Key #2

Read this: Piano Lessons - Book 1: The Hal Leonard Student Piano Library. It's a great beginner piano book available in paperback form on Amazon for about $8.

HOW PIANO BUILDS A FOUNDATION

Playing the piano teaches skills that easily cross over to your primary instrument. It's so useful for beginners that I would recommend it as the first instrument for all kids under five.

First of all, it's a great instrument on which to learn about rhythm and pitch. You can't beat the piano for sight singing practice, either. It also helps you learn to read two clefs. The thing that I like best about studying the piano, however, is the way it improves the coordination between your hands.

Playing an instrument isn't like spiking volleyballs or swinging a baseball bat. Unlike many other physical activities, it requires you to split the attention you pay to your hands. When you spike a volleyball, nearly all of your focus is directed to the spiking hand. When you swing a baseball bat, both hands are doing the exact same thing. When you play the piano *(or the violin or most other instruments)*, your hands are performing different tasks simultaneously. This demands a special type of skill, and the piano nurtures it beautifully.

SHOULD YOU TAKE PRIVATE LESSONS?

When I went to college, I was almost as bad playing the piano as I was singing. I had no experience whatsoever and I turned out fine.

But is "fine" good enough? Are private lessons something you should consider?

My position is always the same: your primary instrument is your primary instrument. There is no doubt that most of your time and effort should be spent building up your technical skill in that area. If your schedule is full, don't worry about piano lessons. You'll learn what you need to learn in your first two years of college.

What I recommend is a mere introduction. Spend a little time on the bench, feel the keys, listen to the different notes, and get familiar with a few basic melodies. Paying particular attention to rhythm and pitch, just learn enough to sit down and play a little bit.

Even when you are in college, you don't need to be a master pianist. You only need to be competent. If you reach that base level before day one, it'll take a little bit of work off your plate. That's the "real world" benefit to getting comfortable ahead of time.

It may seem a little backwards, but the closer you get to college without learning the piano, the less I would worry about it. It pays greater dividends the earlier you start. If you're in middle school or early high school, a few lessons might not be a bad idea, though. As long as you play a little bit from time to time, you're bound to remember enough that two years of piano will be a piece of cake.

If you're in your junior or senior year, you should probably be beyond basic skills *(at least with your primary instrument)*. Learning the piano is a good thing, but not so important that you should sacrifice time with your primary instrument to do it. Just wait until college. You're going to have to take those classes anyway.

If you insist on getting your feet wet for personal reasons, I would probably just stick to a cheap lesson book and a few instructional videos online. You don't want to go out and buy a piano just for this, either. A keyboard will introduce you to the elementary stuff for now.

Key #3: Take All the Music Classes

Depending on how much your school values the arts, you may have the opportunity to take one or more academic music classes. If you are fortunate enough to have such an opportunity, do not waste it.

The most common music class you'll find in high school is AP Music Theory. Whether you're used to taking advanced classes or not, this is not one you want to pass up. AP Music Theory will introduce you to many of the skills and concepts you're going to have to know as a college student. You'll learn notational, compositional, and analytic skills that allow you to document, create, and explore music. You will also be exposed to a bunch of fundamental ideas and terminology *(such as meter, melodic construction, intervals, cadences, phrase structure, etc.)* that will help you learn and talk about music. Another perk is that it will probably be your introduction to sight singing.

Tip for Key #3

Download this: The AP Counselor/Teacher Conversation Starter. This 4-page .pdf walks you through the process of signing up for AP Music Theory. You can find it easily by searching "AP counselor teacher conversation starter" on your favorite search engine.

Understanding music theory is what makes you a musician. Anybody can learn to make sounds with an instrument. Knowing how, when, and why is what sets professionals apart.

If you need more convincing, here's a personal story that might inspire you to make the smart choice and sign up for some music classes next year.

DAY ONE: DEAD LAST

I did not take any theory classes in high school and regretted it on my very first day in college. It was a chilly autumn day when I arrived in class and found a seat among two dozen other music majors. We were all 18-20 years old and more than a few of us looked a little nervous.

It turns out only one of us had reason to be.

After spending a few minutes in the room, right as the chatter of a few friendly groups began to take hold, the professor walked in. He introduced himself as Professor Miguel Roig-Francoli and I later learned that he was a successful Spanish composer and academic. I remember thinking that he looked the part.

He was ready to get down to business and quickly began the first lesson. Turning to the class, he shrugged and asked, "who knows what a seventh chord is?" I didn't know the answer, but wasn't too worried. He was just leading into the first lesson – it wouldn't get difficult yet.

Right?

As I was reassuring myself, hands shot up all over the classroom. I looked around. I was the only student without his hand in the air. A few students were looking my way. One guy wore a look of pity.

The new professor surveyed the classroom, nodding. Satisfied with the knowledge of his new students, he promptly began to teach.

He never actually explained what a seventh chord was. The lesson ended before I knew it and that was as close I as ever got to being on top of things. I never caught up and failed my first semester of theory. I took it again and passed with no problem, but things sure would have been easier if I'd taken it in high school.

Key #4: Study Theory on Your Own

The classroom setting offers structure, a variety of perspectives, and a teacher who can answer your questions. That's why you should take formal theory classes if your school offers them.

More important than the classroom, though, is that you learn the theory. You don't need the teacher. You don't need the classmates. You need the knowledge – and it's everywhere.

Tip for Key #4

Visit here: www.EdX.org. EdX offers free college courses from the top universities in the world. Sign up for an ongoing or an archived course and learn college level music theory from a real college professor while you're still in high school.

Today, an Amazon search returns over 106,000 books when you type in the words "music theory." When you read this book, there will almost certainly be more. If you go to YouTube and type in the same phrase, you immediately are provided with "about 3,480,000 results."

Don't get stressed out about it, though. While there's a lot to learn, there's not three and a half million videos' worth of knowledge you'll have to process. Just buy a book or watch a few videos per week and you'll begin developing a base of knowledge that you can grow over time. One of the best things about studying theory independently is that you can spend your time learning about the aspects of it that are most interesting to you. That's how the best learning happens anyway.

Key #5: Support Other Musicians

The arts survive because people continue to support artists and the excellent work that they're doing. As a future professional musician, you need to be out there supporting your peers whenever you can.

Make it a point to attend the performances of your friends. Purchase albums *(or singles)* that you enjoy. Spread the word about good work on your blog and social media channels. At the very least, make a point to say nice things when you can.

Tip for Key #5

Be friendly: Send a supportive social media message to one fellow musician per week. They can be classmates, friends, or strangers. Not sure what to say? Start with "I heard you play the other day. You were really great!" It's that easy.

Supporting other musicians may not seem like an important aspect of your preparation, but there are at least three good reasons to do it.

1. YOU CAN LIFT THE WHOLE

When you show up in the audience of a friend's performance, you're not just being a good friend. You're being a good musician too.

Although we think about music as art, it is also its own sort of culture. You can contribute to that culture with the cost of a ticket or the thunder of applause. The performances at schools and venues in your neighborhood are counting on the local population for support. That's where your influence can be the strongest.

I will admit that it's sometimes difficult to think that you can have any influence at all. When that happens, I do two things.

First, I consider how good it makes me feel when people I know take time out of their lives to come listen to me perform. *(That always makes me feel warm and fuzzy.)* Second, I remember this old John Donne poem [1]:

---

1 "No Man is An Island" by John Donne, 1624. In the Olde English version there were lots of words spelled differently, but this version is modernized so that it doesn't look so weird.

No man is an island entire of itself; every man

is a piece of the continent, a part of the main;

if a clod be washed away by the sea, Europe

is the less, as well as if a promontory were, as

well as any manner of thy friends or of thine

own were; any man's death diminishes me,

because I am involved in mankind.

And therefore never send to know for whom

the bell tolls; it tolls for thee.

Each and every one of us is part of the whole and when we do something good for the music community, everyone benefits.

2. IT'S GOOD FOR YOUR KARMA

I'm not going to get too deep here, but you're a pretty big hypocrite if you want support without supporting others. You reap what you sow.

3. HELPING OTHERS TODAY CAN HELP YOU TOMORROW

An important idea that I hope you'll remember is that it's okay to think of yourself. There's no harm in wondering "how will this benefit me?"

This is true when it comes to supporting other musicians too. Participating in the musical activities, projects, and performances of your friends and neighbors doesn't just need to be a selfless act. You're allowed to get something out of it too, and I'm not talking about the enjoyment of the music *(although that's obviously a perk).*

When you support the work of other musicians, let people know. I mean, don't be a jerk about it, but try to find other people like you.

If you can find like-minded people, you may be able to develop relationships that can pay off down the line. I've known friends to find mentors and future collaborative partners just by making themselves available while they support other musicians. They find a way to strike up conversations with performers or attendees and form useful contacts.

In this business, you spend most of your time as your own salesman, so don't be afraid to make an impression on someone who might be willing to make a "purchase" down the line.

Networking Made Easy

Networking seems like a daunting task for most people, but it's the only way to nurture relationships. It's common for us to fall into the habit of only talking to people when we need something from them. That is not a form of networking.

In my experience, call-you-when-I-need-you relationships quickly wither and die. No one wants to feel like you only stay in contact with them so you can get something. People want to be treated like people. I know it's a weird thing to write but it's so true. Let me share some of the things that I do to keep my relationships strong:

- I try to contact anyone in my sphere of influence at least once monthly, just to see how they are and how everything is going.
- I treat every one of those people like friends.
- I pay attention to news and social media to see if there is anything special happening for my friends, so I can congratulate them on their success or to let them know that I think what they are doing is fantastic.
- I am always there if they need to bounce ideas around or if they want advice about something that they are thinking about doing *(maybe an upcoming project or a possible change to how they run their festival).*
- I let them know how important they are to me and how grateful I

am to have them in my life.

- I remember that these are long lasting friendships that I want to have, not merely stepping stones to the next job or the next gig.
- I really do like to talk on the phone. I feel like snail mail was the first dying art form of my lifetime. Now, even talking to somebody on the phone seems to be a thing of the past, but that's still how I prefer to communicate. I pick up the phone once a month and call my friends just to make sure that they're doing well and that everything is all right. It goes a long way.

It's important for people to know that you are invested in them and it's not all about you. There is nothing more off-putting than repeatedly getting that same old phone call from the same old guy, asking whether you know of any new gigs. That's something that friends might do from time to time, but it's not the only thing they do.

Your first meeting

The very first time I meet someone I make sure that the conversation is all about them. I like to ask them questions to show that I am genuinely interested in what they have to say. I don't rush the conversation. I don't hurry them along. I carry on the conversation for as long as they are willing to talk to me.

In the initial conversation, I never talk about myself, unless they ask me specific questions. Why do I do that? Two reasons: The first is that I like to see if they are genuinely interested in me at all. If they are, they'll eventually ask me a few questions. The second is that I want to know whether the person I'm talking to is the type of person that loves to talk about him- or herself. See, if they are genuinely interested in me, then the conversation will be very easy and free flowing. I ask them a question and then they turn around and ask me a question. That's how relationships grow. On the other hand, if the conversation never steers away from them, then I know that is how that relationship would always be.

Redefining "networking"

Somehow, the word "networking" has become associated with emotionless, you-scratch-my-back-I-scratch-yours relationships. That's not how it has to be.

If you can start thinking about networking as the building of long-term friendships, then you will be much better off. That's why networking has been so much easier for me to comprehend than it is for many other people. Everything I do with music or my business stems from the idea that we are all in it together.

Friends want to be able to relate to one another and share success stories and failure stories with one another. I like that. If you don't have friends, you don't have anyone you can bounce ideas off of, ask questions of, or celebrate with – and that just doesn't sound like much fun to me.

Key #6: Work the Summer

This one is really important, so I want to be very clear: playing your instrument is not like riding a bike. You don't walk away for a while and then pick right back up where you left off. Reaching a professional level requires constant attention and continued skill development.

That's why it is so important to continue working hard all year. I don't care how good you are, three months away from your instrument is suicide. I've been playing my violin for more than 20 years and I feel rusty if I don't pick it up for a long weekend. There's no way you can put it down for the whole summer and come back without serious loss of ability.

TIP FOR KEY #6

Attend a camp: Sign up for a camp. In the appendix, I've included a résumé template to make it easier. In chapter 4, I'll explain what to do (and when to do it), so you can get into a great camp/festival.

As a teenager, summer still holds a sort of magic, but you cannot allow yourself to sit around and do nothing. When you're working towards a professional music career, summer isn't the time to relax.

In fact, summer is when you should be making the largest gains. As soon as class time is removed from your schedule, you immediately have a minimum of 35 extra hours every week. What are you going to do with it?

Even if you do take a summer class, attend frequent club meetings, and compete in year-round athletics, you're going to have plenty of time to focus on music. And you absolutely should.

Here's what I recommend…

RAMP UP YOUR LESSONS

During the school year, your focus is pulled in a dozen different directions. You're studying chemical elements, the War of 1812, The Adventures of Huckleberry Finn, trigonometry, the digestive system, and how to conjugate Spanish verbs, and that's before you even consider picking up your instrument.

In the summertime, all *(or nearly all)* of those other subjects are taken off your plate. With fewer distractions, you can focus more of your energy on lessons. That makes your summer lessons far more valuable than those you take during the school year.

Take advantage of it.

As long as you can afford to do it, take another lesson or two each week. Talk to your instructor and make it clear that you want to dedicate extra effort and extra time to your instrument. If you have particular goals in mind, share them. If there are technical shortcomings that are holding you back, practice them specifically. Any good instructor will happily plan lessons that can make the most of your additional efforts.

Take Instrument-Friendly Vacations

Many families take a few weeks in the summer to step away from their responsibilities, have fun, and enjoy each other's company. I think that's great. Vacation is a good thing. The problem with vacations is that most students think that it's also a vacation from practice. It's not.

If I took two or three weeks off from practice, it would take me another month to get back into violin shape. My summer would be wasted! That will be even truer for you, having played many fewer years than I have.

Because summer is an opportunity for you to make big gains in a short period, you need to continue practicing even while you're on vacation. Let your parents know that any vacation you take needs to include your instrument. If they don't like it, explain that you want to continue growing and that skipping practice will knock you way off track. Your parents will appreciate your commitment.

ATTEND A CAMP

Another thing I recommend for young musicians is to attend a music camp. There are day camps and overnight camps, where attendants remain onsite for the length of the program. Seminars and lessons are facilitated by professionals who are comfortable working with young performers, and the camp generally ends with at least one performance that is open to the public.

Depending on the reputation of a particular camp, simply signing up may not be enough to get you in. Worthwhile camps with limited availability will hold auditions to determine who gets each spot. Strong programs often offer tuition discounts or scholarships to skilled students who cannot otherwise afford to attend.

Attending a music camp is not the same as private lessons, and there are lots of reasons why it is a good idea to participate in one.

Here are some ways camp can help you:

Exposure to New Mentors

Whenever you pursue any activity, hobby, or career, you can assume that there is at least one person better than you are. If you can find that person, it is wise to listen to what they have to say. Experienced people that have already walked your path can advise you how to find success without struggling like they did.

Music camps are full of students and instructors who are likely to be more skilled than you are, and that's a good thing. There's an old adage that says, "good artists copy; great artists steal." Well, when you are at music camp, I want you to "steal" all the knowledge that you can get your hands on.

It will make you a better and smarter musician.

Strong Focus & Constant Feedback

There is only one purpose to any decent music camp: make the students better.

Camps succeed in this regard because everyone has the same focus. From the director to the newest attendee, everyone's head is in the same place. That makes camp a great place to grow musically, even if the growth only occurs as a result of mistakes.

For the limited time that you are attending camp, the instructors' main goal is to improve your skills. If you're playing a note poorly, they'll help you fix it. If your timing seems off, they'll help you fix it. If you aren't grasping how a section is supposed to sound, they'll help you fix it.

New Friends and Partners

Selective camps attract musicians from all over the place. Surrounding yourself with other young musicians broadens your circle of possible contacts and increases the chances that you form strong relationships.

I cannot promise you that these relationships will develop into collaborations or other profitable ventures. What I can promise you is that – even if they don't – creating friendships with musical people like yourself promotes creativity and provides new perspectives.

Personally, I've been fortunate enough to forge some important relationships during my time at music camps. One friendship really stands out.

It was in the early 2000s and I was attending the Aspen Music Festival. With me was a fellow violinist who I hadn't yet met. Her name was Jinjoo Cho, and she was only 12 years old. She was born in Korea and hadn't yet learned much English, but Jinjoo was terrifically nice – and one heck of a violinist! We enjoyed each other's company, and I learned a lot about my instrument watching her play.

Today, she has a laundry list of awards, including the 2014 Gold Medal of the Ninth Quadrennial International Violin Competition, held in Indianapolis. *(Her impressive career is well-documented online if you want to learn more about it.)*

Fortunately, we recently ended up reconnecting. It turns out that we both host our own festivals. Because we already know each other, we're comfortable bouncing ideas off one another, providing support, and participating in each other's festivals as instructors. Our relationship isn't just friendly, but also professional.

And all of that came about because we met at a music camp.

A Whole Lot of Fun

Since you are looking for a career, you should know that there are "fun" camps and there are "serious" camps. The fun camps are good places to make new friends and enjoy your time. The serious camps are where you go to become a better musician.

I always, always recommend going to the most "serious" camp you can get into, but don't think it's all work and no fun. When you surround yourself with talented people that have the same long-term goals as you do, you're bound to have a good time, no matter how tough the lessons might be.

Your first résumé

When you're applying for summer festivals or are getting ready to apply for colleges, you'll need to have a résumé handy. No matter what program it is you're trying to get into, the gatekeepers will want to know what kind of experience you have. Have you played solo performances? Have you ever played in the pit? You know – that sort of thing.

That's why, starting in your freshman year, you want to start keeping records. It's a good idea to keep a list of all your performances. If you can save the programs, that's a nice touch. Save all the relevant documents in a binder that you can use to formulate a résumé down the road.

I know that this is excellent advice, because it's something that I failed to do. No one ever explained to me that I would need to tell people everything I'd done. It wasn't until I applied to teach at a college that someone finally asked me for a résumé. It took me weeks to track down the details of my important performances. Even then, I know that I left off a few shows that would have really made good additions.

Nowadays, camps and colleges ask students for their résumés all the time. You can save yourself a whole lot of stress and trouble by having yours ready to go.

SOME AWESOME 18 & UNDER CAMPS TO CONSIDER

All over the country *(and the world)*, you'll find excellent music camps that will challenge and inspire you. To give you an idea of what to look for, I'm going to provide you with the names and locations of ten awesome camps. They're from all over the United States, plus one from Europe. *(If you're wondering which one is the very best, then I guess I need to point you to Texas Strings Festival, the strings-specific camp I've been operating in Austin since 2015!)*

- Texas Strings Festival in Austin, Texas

- Encore Chamber Music and Academy, near Cleveland, Ohio
- Tanglewood Music Center in Western Massachusetts
- Music Academy of the West in Santa Barbara, California
- Aspen Music Festival in Aspen, Colorado
- IMS Prussia Cove in London, UK
- Music@Menlo, near San Jose, California
- Meadowmount School of Music in Northern New York
- Perlman Music Program in New York City
- Yellow Barn Music Festival in Southern Vermont

I just want to remind you that these are not the only worthwhile camps out there. There are loads of others that can give you everything you need. The important thing is that you find one that works for you.

Key #7: Relearn How to Practice

In the first lessons you ever took, your teacher told you how important practice was. If you played what you learned a few times each day, you would memorize it and become a skilled musician. Sounds easy, right?

Well, by now you should know that mere repetition isn't always enough to grow. It's great for kids and absolute beginners because drilling engrains the movements into your memory and beginners need that foundation to build on. As you get better, you need to develop new practice methods that use your knowledge and stretch your ability. That's how you grow.

You probably are not receiving regular practice instruction, so I'm going to give you 6 Pointers for Perfect Practice. If you follow my advice, you will learn new material easily and perform beautifully.

Tip for Key #7

Schedule tomorrow: You might not have a practice journal yet, but don't let that stop you. Put this book down, grab a piece of scrap paper and write tomorrow's practice schedule. Be specific, and account for every minute. (You can make your own practice journal using a composition book and a pencil, but if you want prompted entries, reflection questions, and professional organization, you can check out my 3-month practice workbook, Quarter Notes.)

Pointer #1: Prepare Your Body

Few people think of it this way, but playing an instrument is a physical activity. Sure, you're engaging your brain, but the music cannot flow without the help of your body.

Before you begin any practice session, audition, or performance, I recommend you ready your body *(and your mind)* with some stretching and deep breathing. These activities increase blood flow, flexibility, and strength. That's exactly what you want before you begin playing for any length of time.

Depending on how long you are expecting to play in a single shot, you may have to remain seated for an hour or more. Sitting too long can decrease circulation, boost insulin production, and tighten up your muscles. If you start your practice sessions with a good stretch, your body can resist these negative effects longer.

Pointer #2: Execute Goal-Focused Practice

There is no worse kind of practice for the would-be professional musician than mindless repetition. It's true that repetition can help build mental and muscle memory, but that's only useful if you're playing perfectly. If there are flaws in the way that you're performing a piece, thoughtlessly playing it over and over will cement those mistakes into your routine permanently.

That's why you should never practice without specific goals in mind.

Goals are excellent motivators and they also provide you the opportunity to see your progress, if you use them correctly. All proper goals have five characteristics. They are specific, measurable, actionable, realistic, and time-oriented. *(It spells SMART, get it?)* If your goals don't have all five of those characteristics, then they aren't helping you get better.

Here's an example of a poor goal and a SMART goal.

Poor goal: I want to learn to play Vivaldi's The Four Seasons.

SMART goal: I will learn how to play the first 25 measures of Vivaldi's The Four Seasons before the end of the month in three steps; I will learn the notes without bowings or rhythms, learn the rhythms without the bowings, and, finally, I will combine it all together.

Do you see the difference? In the first goal, the musician has only a broad idea of what he or she wants to accomplish. The second goal reveals a specific, measurable, actionable, realistic, time-oriented goal that lays out exactly how it will be achieved. There's no doubt as to what happens next.

That's how you should plan your practice.

I recommend using a full sheet of paper to document each of your goals. At the top, record the name for your goal. A good name for ours could be "The Four Seasons – 25 measures." Then divide the sheet into three sections and label them "What," "How," and "When." Under "What," state exactly what it is you want to achieve. Use as many details as possible, especially if numbers, grades, or ratings are involved. Under "How," list all steps you'll need to complete to achieve your goal. Under "When," write the date of your deadline, including any major checkpoints you'll want to hit along the way. If you include checkpoints, provide specific dates for each of them, as well.

Documenting your goals creates a record of your commitments and gives you an accurate idea of how to go about meeting them.

Pointer #3: Record & Analyze Your Performances

Have you ever heard a recording of your own voice and been surprised by the way you really sound? The same thing can happen with your instrument. to get an accurate idea of how well you're playing, you need to get "outside your head" and hear it as if you were a total stranger.

Nowadays, recording yourself playing your instrument is super easy. You can record yourself using your smartphone, tablet, or computer. When you're finished playing, put your instrument down and listen to your recording.

As you listen, pay attention to the details. Did you cut a note short too soon? Are you playing a section more harshly than you should? These types of observations reveal the tiny changes that make a big difference. It's a good idea to listen to the recording a few times in a row. Use one playback to observe tempo and another to focus on pitch. Breaking down your work this way lets you hone in on specific characteristics and how to fix them. That can be difficult to do if you only think about them while playing your instrument.

If you really want to get the most out of this suggestion, here's a pro tip: make notes of your observations and keep them in a safe place. You'll likely notice patterns that indicate where you have the most room for improvement. *(Combine this tip with the next pointer for best results.)*

Pointer #4: Maintain a Practice Journal

Another one of my favorite practice tools is the practice journal. Keeping a practice journal is a good way to keep track of skills you want to practice and an even better way to incorporate them into your practice routine.

I like to make four kinds of notes in my practice journal.

Schedule Entries

When you pick up a practice journal, the first thing you should do is write down the next time you're going to practice and what you plan to work on. I call this a schedule entry and it looks like this:

Tomorrow, November 15th, I will practice for 3 hours and I will spend:

- 45 minutes on A major scale, allotting:
- 10 minutes to the shifts on the A string and E string in the scale
- 10 minutes to tone, listening for evenness and deepness throughout the bow
- 3 minutes for 8 to the bow
- 12 minutes to the top octave of the scale
- 10 minutes to clarity of left hand articulation
- And all remaining time to the piece assigned by my instructor

Schedule entries provide structure and organization, allowing you to focus on things that need your attention.

Review Entries

After I've finished practicing for the day, I sometimes like to make notes about the success or failure of my session. If certain movements are giving me trouble, I will document the difficulty. If I make a realization worth remembering, I'll write that down too. I won't get too technical *(that's for the next type of entry)*, but I will make quick notes that I can reference easily later.

Review entries are valuable because they allow me to track details that I thought were important while playing, but would probably forget otherwise.

Analysis Entries

One of my earlier practice recommendations was to record and analyze your own performances. The problem is that merely listening to what you played doesn't accomplish much. Analysis entries encourage you to move from vague assessments into productive critiques.

When you really do it seriously, analysis entries will be the product of careful listening, detailed criticism, and thoughtful advice for correcting problems.

Goal Entries

If you're practicing with goals in mind, it can be useful to write them down. When you try to store them in your head, you get fuzzy on the details and the goals become useless. Write them down and remember to make them specific, measurable, actionable, realistic, and time-oriented. I offered a useful template for goal-writing in Pointer #2.

Pointer #5: Don't Measure Success in Hours

Many hard-working musicians end up developing more slowly than they should because they cannot get past the idea that they are supposed to practice some arbitrary number of hours each day. They spend hour after hour playing their instrument, but don't pay attention to anything other than the clock on the wall.

This is a mistake. Practicing with an emphasis on time doesn't produce results. It produces tendonitis. What you need to focus on is technique and understanding why certain methods create a more beautiful sound.

The thing that I really want to stress is that it doesn't matter how long you practice if you're practicing the wrong way. I'd much rather you practice well for one hour each day than to mindlessly play the same piece over and over for ten – and I bet you would too. When you follow the first five pointers, you'll get far better results in far less time.

Pointer #6: Find a Lesson Buddy

You're probably beginning to understand that practicing deliberately is about more than simply playing the notes. It's a mental process that only succeeds when you really engage your brain. That's what all this practice advice is really about. It's about getting your brain involved in the process.

One way you can do that is by finding yourself a lesson buddy. A lesson buddy is a partner that you work with during lessons or practice sessions. This is how it works.

You pair up with a classmate or friend who is studying the same instrument you are. It works best when you and your partner have approximately the same abilities. When you have a private lesson, your buddy comes along and observes with a notebook. During your lesson, the buddy quietly takes notes critiquing your performance, commending your strengths, and highlighting areas you need to improve. You now have an honest account of your work from a third party.

You can use these notes to adjust your goals, alter your practice schedule, or simply evaluate your skills.

Obviously, you'll need to attend your buddy's lessons and offer the same critique. That's why I love lesson buddies so much. It's a dedicated partnership that not only improves students' performances, but also strengthens their ability to review, critique, and solve problems. Lesson buddies are so important that I use them with all my students.

If you cannot manage to attend one another's lessons, the lesson buddy system also works for at-home practice. Just be careful not to become distracted!

Key #8: Get Your Money in Order

One of the most important things you can do for your future self is to learn how to handle money. It's easy to think that you'll be fine, but the truth of the matter is that most people in America are only "fine" if you set the bar very low.

Americans are bad with money. They spend too much, save too little, and are rarely prepared to handle any expense that's not part of their monthly routine. I could get super specific and hit you with a bunch of depressing statistics, but I prefer to keep it upbeat. Instead, I'll just leave you with this surprising fact:

63% of Americans do not have enough money saved to pay for a $500 emergency expense. [2]

---

2 http://www.forbes.com/sites/maggiemcgrath/2016/01/06/63-of-americans-dont-have-enough-savings-to-cover-a-500-emergency/#554d8a876dde

As a teenager, $500 might seem like a whole lot of money, but I promise you that it's not. It's a trip to the vet, a set of used tires for your car, a two-hour visit from the plumber to fix a surprise leak. If you want to be able to handle these common emergencies as an adult, you need to start learning fiscal responsibility today.

The other important thing to remember is that most Americans are working regular 9-5 jobs that deliver steady paychecks and they still cannot manage a surprise $500 expense. For the musician who doesn't have a weekly paycheck coming in, managing money can be even harder.

Tip for Key #8

Sign up: A free account at Mint.com will change your life. It tracks all your spending, bills (if you have any), and savings. It lets you set financial goals and will even update you when bill and goal deadlines are approaching.

While you're in middle or high school, you're probably not making much *(if any)* money at all, but that doesn't mean it's too early to start learning about how to get your finances in order. In fact, it's probably the best time. If you learn a few basic principles now, you're more likely to carry them with you into your professional career.

I have three recommendations for young people who want to start getting money-smart:

1. SAVE IMMEDIATELY

If you're ever going to have enough money to make a big purchase or cover an emergency expense, you're going to have to save. The best way to do this is to save "off the top." If you're working a part-time job and earn $60 this week, put fifteen or twenty dollars into a savings account right away. If you make this habit automatic *(which is easy to do if you have an employer who allows direct deposit of your paycheck)*, then you never have to suffer the painful act of forking it over later.

Once you accumulate some savings, you might want to look into investing, but the way to start is just to practice not spending it all.

2. CREATE A BUDGET

Ask someone how much money they spend on food each month, and they probably don't know. The same is true of most other expenses. Creating a budget allows you to track your spending, identify patterns, and make smarter choices.

You can do it easily with a notepad, electronic spreadsheets, or free online budgeting software like Mint.

3. THINK LONG-TERM

We all have the tendency to do what benefits us right now. When it comes to money, we must fight that urge. Poor short-term decisions that hurt us down the road include:

- Spending money on credit cards
- Ignoring grant/scholarship opportunities
- Paying bills late
- Outspending our earnings
- Refusing to save

When I say it like that, it's probably easy to agree with my assessment. It gets hard when the decisions force you to choose between going to see a movie with friends or depositing the $15 you committed to save. Make smart decisions now and you'll be grateful down the road, especially if the refrigerator breaks.

Your 8 Keys to Future Success

I don't want to sound like a broken record, but this chapter is a goldmine of practical advice. Follow my recommendations and you'll be lightyears ahead of your peers mentally.

Just so you don't forget, here are the 8 Keys to Future Success, one more time:

1. Start sight singing
2. Try your hand at piano
3. Take music classes
4. Study theory
5. Support musicians
6. Work all summer
7. Relearn practice
8. Get money-smart

I've said it several times, and I'll say it again. Implement my advice and you will be the only one with their head in the right place. From there, all you'll have to do is get into college!

We'll cover that in the next chapter.

CHAPTER 4

EVERY PARENT'S FAVORITE TOOL: THE STRINGS SUCCESS TIMETABLE

So much to do, so little time.

One of the biggest problems facing young musicians is the sheer volume of advice that they receive. From parents to friends, teachers to guidance counselors, everywhere you turn, there's someone else ready to chime in with their two cents. Although nearly all of it is well-intentioned, these suggestions are presented in a haphazard way. With so much to do to prepare for college, random advice isn't good enough. They need a blueprint that details not just what to do, but when to do it.

With that in mind, I created the Strings Success Timetable. In this chapter, I break down - month by month - the tasks that any college bound strings musician should be completing during his or her high school years.

More than just a pile of advice, the timetable gives you clear instructions describing what needs to be done and when you should get started. It also gives you plenty of lead time, so that you can complete every task well before your deadlines arrive. In it, I explain when is the best time to address overlooked issues and when your priorities need to begin shifting. If you follow it closely, you'll position yourself for success without any surprises.

Before we get started, there's just one more thing. Unlike other sections, this chapter is a sort of checklist. That means that most of the attention will be set on the "what" as opposed to the "how" and "why." Of course, I will give you some explanation as to how to accomplish each task, but I'm going to keep everything concise.

There will be some stuff I want to discuss in more detail, though. Those discussions are located in the next two chapters of the book, "How to Become an Attractive Candidate for Colleges" and "Selecting Your School."

In the meantime, I present the Strings Success Timetable.

Trying New Things in Your Freshman Year

As a freshman, you're probably realizing that music is your preferred career choice. Even if you're not 100% certain, you want to start making the preparations now. When you decide that string instruments are your future, you don't want to scramble just to be ready.

Fall Semester

Evaluate your teacher

The first thing you need to do is determine whether your private instructor is up for the task of getting you into a college's music program. Not all teachers have good track records when it comes to preparing students for the college application, prescreening, and audition process. Find an instructor who knows what it takes and start taking lessons now. It could take a few weeks, or even months, to get familiar with the new teacher's dynamic.

Spring Semester

Expand your repertoire

The string repertoire is vast and you'll be expected to have mastered a certain portion of it before colleges are likely to accept you. Expanding your repertoire exposes you to different styles of music from different periods and composers. The more you know, the greater your understanding of the "language" of composition.

Juggle new pieces

Once you've begun to expand your repertoire a little bit, try to prepare different pieces at the same time. In college, you won't have the luxury of preparing the same periods of music at the same time. You may need to play pieces from the Baroque, Classical, and Romantic eras, all in a single recital. Familiarizing yourself with this process while you're still young can be of great value to you later. *(Just don't beat yourself up if it's too hard when you first get started.)*

Battling the Sophomore Slump

Fall Semester

Look beyond the lull

As a sophomore, your college auditions are both a long way off and right around the corner. You should be using this time to build, build, build your repertoire. In your junior year, your focus will be mostly on perfecting what you already know, so use this time to learn everything you can.

Plan your schedule

Sophomore year is the year of the rough patch. You want to do well musically and academically, without sacrificing a social life. This can be difficult. You want to dedicate some time to planning your schedule, figuring out how much time you need to succeed in all areas of your life. It is often a good idea to discuss your schedule with parents or guidance counselors when you're feeling stressed or falling behind.

Spring Semester

Keep on learning

If you have any say in the matter, try to plan your most difficult classes in the fall, so that things start to lighten up in the spring. That way you can begin to double down on practice. With the summer quickly approaching, you'd like to get to peak practicing condition as soon as possible. Continue filling your repertoire with new material and prepare for a busy summer.

Preparations and Evaluations: Your Junior Year

September

Make a List of Schools

In your junior year, it's really time to start looking forward. All throughout this year, you'll be chipping away at the overwhelming world of music education to narrow down your plans. The first thing you can do is start compiling a list of possible schools.

You may not know which schools suit you best, so it's okay to use friends, family, teachers, counselors, and the internet for help. The one thing you really want to figure out, though, is whether to go the conservatory or college/university route. These institutions educate their students in different ways. You must figure out which is better suited for you. *(Answers to your questions about the difference between them can be found in chapter 6, "Selecting Your School.")*

Ask "Big Picture" Questions

There are other major factors that can influence your decision to attend a school. Things like weather, distance from home, proximity to cultural hubs, and cost of living all help determine your final decision. Answer some of the big picture questions now and you won't waste time researching them more thoroughly later.

Get Some Data

Some questions are best answered with hard facts. Find out how much student aid is available and whether you qualify. Look into student graduation rates. Do most students graduate on time? What is the total cost of tuition, when you include room & board, meal plans, and transportation?

Getting numbers is one way to make black-and-white comparisons between two schools.

Research Their Programs

Once you've compiled a list of preliminary schools, start looking at their programs. You can often knock schools right off the list simply by checking whether they are strong in the areas on which you want to focus. Knowing that you want an orchestral career over a chamber career, for instance, can help you eliminate all the schools without a strong orchestral component.

Good programs present students with opportunities to develop and prosper. Masterclasses with experts, solo performances, and chamber music performances are just some of the opportunities that could pare down your list.

October

Research Prospective Teachers

When it comes to considering prospective teachers, it's okay to turn into a bit of a detective. I believe that your teacher is the most important factor of all when it comes to selecting a school, so you definitely don't want to pick one on a whim.

A good thing to consider is the ratio of undergrad students to master's and doctoral students. Just like some grade school teachers prefer elementary over high school, some college music teachers prefer to teach students of a certain level. Knowing where they stand on this issue could make things easier for you.

Get the Nitty Gritty

Another thing you want to look at is the frequency of lessons. Some teachers maintain busy concert careers. If their own performances take them out of town, you may not have a lesson for a few weeks at a time.

Also, do your best to speak with their current or former students. Students will know what the learning experience is like, and are generally willing to share their experiences. Ask them about lesson frequency, performance opportunities, and whether they're getting help finding a job. Students can also provide invaluable information about a teacher's style and attitude.

Seek Out First-Hand Experiences

When you believe you have found a teacher that matches your needs, do what you can to get a lesson. This person is going to be your mentor for years. Don't you think it's a good idea to spend at least one lesson with them before committing?

Here's a really good idea: try to get into the summer music festival(s) that your preferred teachers are operating. If you're accepted, you'll get extended, first hand exposure to them.

November

Let the Information Marinate

Most of November is going to be spent on the lookout for summer music festivals, but that doesn't mean you should cast all the other stuff aside. Let it marinate in your mind. Occasionally refer to your informational materials, and never stop asking questions. You don't have to dig in deep, but never let it disappear fully. Sometimes, the right choice makes itself apparent when you just take a step back.

Start the Festival Hunt

A music festival is the best way for you to spend your summer, because you get advanced instruction and zero distractions. Every serious high school musician should attend at least one per year.

I suggest you get festival recommendations from your private instructor. Your instructor knows your plans and your abilities, allowing them to simplify the search a little bit. Some major things you'll have to ponder are:

- How long do you want to be at a festival? Some are only a week, while others last the entire summer.
- How much can you and your parents afford to spend? Festival costs can run pretty high, though scholarships and financial aid are sometimes available.
- Do you want to work within a certain focus? Soloists may be better suited for one festival over another. The same is true for ensemble, chamber, and orchestral musicians.
- Is there a maximum distance you're willing to travel? Location is obviously a serious factor for most people.

Reach out to former students of the festival too, if you can. People who've been through the experience have insights that will make your decision so much easier. Plus, getting friendly with musicians is just good business.

December

Consider More Sessions

If you're putting in a lot of practice time, then picking up extra lessons could be really valuable to you. Doubling your lessons from one to two hours per week opens lots of opportunities. When my students are ready for a second lesson, I tend to split the time evenly between technique and repertoire.

When you do change your schedule to include a second lesson, find out how your teacher would prefer to structure them. That way you can be prepared.

Explore Performance Options

Practice is great, but the purpose of all our work is to perform! If you pick up an extra lesson, you can use some of that time to perfect your practice repertoire. Once you're satisfied, turn it into your performance repertoire!

Your instructor can help you schedule a performance.

Ready Your Audition Tapes

Pay attention to the application requirements of your favorite festivals and ensure that you are ready when the time comes to submit.

January

Visit Campuses

Back in November, you shifted your attention away from the college selection process, but now is the time to get back to it. Talk with your parents about the need to visit your top college choices and work with them to schedule a visit.

Your parents will need to accompany you on your visit, and they will probably be funding it too. Finding a time that works for them should be your number one priority. Don't underestimate how much they're contributing to your dream. You need their help, so be flexible.

As far as school is concerned, the best time to visit a prospective college is during one of the scheduled breaks. The winter and spring breaks are perfect. They're long enough to string a few visits together in one shot. If this is a viable option for you, your teachers and your parents will appreciate it.

Whenever you figure out the right time to visit, email prospective teachers and try to set up a meeting. The meeting should include a personal conversation and a trial lesson.

Evaluate the Experience

Campus visits are busy, but do what you can to get the full experience. Walk all over the grounds, visit student housing, and venture off-campus. Does the environment appear safe? Will you need a vehicle to navigate the campus and surrounding neighborhoods? Are the people you meet friendly and polite? Is the weather conducive to your personality and/or lifestyle? These are the types of questions you want to try to answer.

It's much easier to study productively if you're comfortable in your environment. When you feel good, you work well.

February

Begin Repertoire Preparation

After a few visits, you should be able to narrow down your list even further. The goal is to get it down to a handful of schools. *(It's a good idea to apply to a safety school, a reach school, and a few you'd expect to be accepted into.)* Once you're down to a handful, it's time to start preparing your repertoire for pre-screenings and auditions.

Research each school's requirements and work with your teacher to begin figuring out what pieces you should be using.

Perform a Skills Self-Assessment

With a roster of pieces in hand, you'll have what amounts to your first professional assignment. You need to be prepared to perform at a high level by an established deadline. Do you have the skills you need to get it done?

An honest assessment of your skills can reveal any foundational shortcomings that need to be addressed. One surefire sign that you need improvements is that it takes you a long time to learn a piece. After you've created an honest self-assessment, bring it to your teacher for review. Tell him or her that you have some areas you want to improve upon, and find out if there are any holes you missed.

Your teacher should then begin hitting on those areas.

Get Organized

Schools have different requirements, teachers, contact information, and deadlines. Balancing it all in your head is nearly impossible, so late February is time to get organized. Create a calendar with all the crucial dates, including your lessons and practice performances. Then, build a resource detailing each school's audition requirements, contact points, and teacher notes.

Once you've got your tools, compare the schools on your list. Try to figure out which pieces will work for multiple auditions. Reusing the same piece can save you a lot of time. If you can showcase those pieces in other performances or competitions, that's a good idea too.

March

Consider an Instrument Upgrade

With some of the most important performances of your life coming up, now is a good time to confirm that your instrument is really what you need. Think back to any feedback you received from your teacher or other musicians you respect. Here are some of the questions you need to answer for yourself:

- Do respectable musicians think the sound is good?
- Does the instrument produce muted sounds?
- Are you struggling to create a different type of tone?
- Can you create the same sounds in a variety of venues?
- Is there inconsistency in the tone, even when your technique is the same?

As usual, it's a good idea to consult with your teacher. An experienced teacher will know whether your instrument is ready to make the jump into college and whether it will last for the next 2-4 years. Take the feedback and make a decision.

April

Shop for a New Instrument (If Required)

Your instrument is like an extension of your own body, so don't just purchase the first one you see. Take your time and shop around.

Shopping around for a new instrument can be a whole lot of fun, as long as you don't overlook the important details. Examine the papers accompanying any instrument you're considering buying, and don't purchase anything without supporting papers describing when it was built, who built it, and its general condition.

The best shops for this will have instruments both in and above your price range. You don't want to spend more than you can afford, but it's nice to have options trade-up options if you want to upgrade later in your career. Some tricky salesmen will try to bait you into purchasing instruments you cannot afford. Stand firm. Do you want a tip? Check the price on every instrument before you start playing it. If you fall in love with an expensive instrument, you and your parents could end up making a foolish financial decision based solely on emotion.

Try It Out

Salesmen have a job to do. They need to sell instruments. Don't let them pressure you into buying anything until you're ready. You have all the time in the world.

Most shops will allow you to take the instrument with you so that you can try it out. When you borrow an instrument, you need to play it in as many places as possible. Big rooms, small rooms, stages, concert halls, dead rooms, wherever you have your lessons. Play it under all reasonable conditions, so that there are no surprises. For the sake of etiquette, though, you shouldn't hold the instrument for more than two weeks.

Take your time before you finally make your purchase. There's no rush. Some people take years before they find the instrument that really works for them.

Don't Forget the Rest

Purchasing an instrument is exciting. I've known people to get so caught up in the fun of it, that they spend their whole budget on the violin and forget that there are more purchases to make!

You must remember to allocate money for your instrument's bow and case. If your instrument doesn't pair nicely with your bow, it's not going to be much use to you. It's also a problem if there's no case in which to store your instrument.

Some Options for Shops

As a violinist, I'm most familiar with the top violin shops, but you can buy other stringed instruments at a few of these shops too. Some of the best around include:

- Reed Yeboah Fine Violins
- John & Arthur Beare
- Rare Violins
- Robertson and Sons
- Reuning and Sons
- Carriage House
- Becker and Sons
- The Potter Violin Company

Each of these shops is recognized by players around the world as carriers of exceptional instruments. The staff at each is incredibly knowledgeable and the prices are fair. Learn more about any of these shops online, and remember to ask your instructor for recommendations in your price range.

Confirm Your Festival(s)

By the end of April, you should know exactly which festival *(or festivals)* you'll be attending in the summer. If you don't know, figure it out quick!

May

Be Social

People are an integral part of your business future. Referrals, jobs, discussions, collaborations – they all come from your relationships. One way to practice forming new relationships is to talk with people on a mutually interesting topic.

As a student preparing to go to college, there are thousands of alumni with whom you share such a topic. Why not talk to them?

This month, I want you to get out there and find alumni and current students from the schools that are still on your list. Whether through the university, human connections, or the internet, find people you can connect with. Ask them the questions you haven't had answered yet. Have them describe their experiences to you in detail. Which courses did or didn't they like? Was the food palatable? Is the alumni association active and useful?

After you've gotten the answers you're looking for, stay in touch! Even low-maintenance connections, like those on social media, can keep you or get you plugged into a network and open up doors.

Have an Honest Look

With the help of personal reviews, even the most attractive schools can begin to look less appealing. Take all the information you've received from visits, conversations, pamphlets, teachers, and students, and give an honest appraisal.

Does this school check enough of your boxes to be a top choice? If not, is it suitable as a backup? Do you need to remove it altogether?

It can be hard to do, but don't get sentimental. If a school isn't going to work for you, you shouldn't go. It doesn't matter that your mom is an alumnus or the teacher really liked your sense of humor. This is business. Make a business decision.

Create Deadlines

You should already be working on your college repertoire, but you should create some deadlines for yourself before you're distracted by summer festivals. Work with your regular teacher to determine how much you should know before the festival starts and how much work you'll need to do after the fact.

Immerse Yourself in Festivals

Once the festival begins, throw yourself into it. This is your last opportunity for rapid growth before you submit your pre-screenings and audition for your top schools. You don't want to throw it away.

You're going to work hard and you're going to have fun. And then you're going to start your senior year of high school.

Pre-screenings, Auditions, and College: Your Senior Year

September

Lessons

In your senior year, you really need to dial up the effort you're pouring into your music. I don't want you to ignore your other studies, but music should become your priority. If that means you need to give up some time on your weekends to make up for lost homework time, so be it.

You need to attend at least two lessons per week.

What would you do if you were an athlete? Would you think that one practice session per week would cut it? I don't think so! Even little leaguers practice 2-3 times per week.

If you want to be good enough to make it into college as a music major, you need to practice, practice, practice.

Recital

Take advantage of this slow period of the year and use it to play a recital of all your college audition pieces. You want to know exactly where you stand and where you need to improve. Might as well find out sooner than later.

With auditions and pre-screenings coming up fast, it's a good idea to have a first study of all pieces. That means playing them back-to-back without stopping. Endurance is an issue here, but you also want to ensure that your rhythm, dynamics, and intonation will last through long performances. Pairing your first study with recital preparations can kill two birds with one stone.

You can work with your instructor to help you set a date and time, find a venue, and set up a recording of your performance.

Finding a Pianist

Another thing to figure out is who you're going to use as your pianist. You'll want to work with the same pianist all year to prepare for pre-screenings. Your pre-screenings are so important, that you can't treat them as a one-off assignment. They require ongoing work, so you'll want a steady partner on the keys.

Here's one piece of advice about picking your pianist: do not select somebody that is learning your music for the first time! It's enough of a burden that you have to learn it. Find a pianist who can already play it expertly, or else you could jeopardize your performances down the road.

Academic Outreach

Get in touch with all the teachers you might like to study under in college and plan to meet them. You want to meet with them before you audition, if possible. Audition season normally lasts from mid-December to early March and is incredibly busy for teachers. If you can manage to make an appointment now, you're more likely to get all their attention. Plus, meeting them outside of your audition window demonstrates your commitment to their program and university.

Review Criteria

If you haven't decided which schools you'll be applying to yet, now's the time. Don't wait any longer. Each school has unique application criteria and if you wait until the last minute, bad things are bound to happen.

Finalize your list of schools and start organizing your pre-screening efforts. The deadlines are usually December 1.

October

Follow Up

If there are any teachers who didn't respond to your last email or letter, follow up. They were probably busy, or just forgot to get back to you. A gentle reminder will bring their attention back to your request to meet them.

A tiny bit of flattery *("I really love the direction you're taking the music program. I would love the opportunity to spend a few minutes with you.")* can go a long way. Just don't overdo it. Nobody likes brown-nosers.

If you're able to open an exchange, make sure to finalize appointment dates and times, and plan your travel. Once your appointment is on the books, work with your private teacher to determine which pieces showcase you best.

Start Rehearsing

With two months left until your pre-screening performances, you should have plenty of time to get things perfect. Work with your pianist regularly and verify that they are totally comfortable with all the music they'll be expected to play for you.

Make Pre-Screening Preparations

Your pre-screening is a big deal. You really do want things to be perfect. Start handling the logistics now so that no issues creep up on you. Some of those details include:

- Finding a venue *(ideally, you want to set up in a concert hall)*
- Hiring an audiovisual technician for recording
- Securing two recording dates
- Scheduling your pianist for the correct dates and times.

Another big part of your preparations is requesting letters of recommendation from all the proper teachers. You want to make those requests in October so that they have plenty of time to organize their thoughts, reflect on your character, and draft a letter that speaks well of you. They probably won't need it, but giving them 4+ weeks prevents you from begging for letters at the last minute.

The final step is obtaining formal attire. Formal clothing sometimes requires alterations that can take a few weeks, so do this sooner than later.

November

Confirm Preparations

Follow up with all your vendors and make sure that your preparations are settled. A thirty second phone call will do the trick.

"Good morning, my name is Pasha Sabouri. I'm just calling to confirm my use of your venue on November 13th." Simple.

Continue Rehearsing

By early November, you should be comfortable with your music. It should really be down to the final touches by now. Your teacher can identify any remaining problems. Now is the time to focus on details. The "big picture" stuff should be second nature by now.

Equipment Check

Don't show up to your pre-screening with faulty equipment.

At the beginning of the month, go over everything. Need new strings? Sound post adjustment? Bow needs to be rehaired? Your instrument needs to be in tip-top shape, so make sure to go over every inch of it.

Record Your Pre-screening

On the day of your pre-screening, eat well, get a good night's sleep, and relax. Every school has different criteria and every teacher looks for specific traits. You won't necessarily know what their particular biases are, so just go out there and play your best. If you follow the blueprint I've laid out for you here and practiced with dedication, you've done everything you can.

Play beautifully and have fun. Just make sure to schedule your recording with plenty of time to do what happens next.

Review and Deliver

Make sure that you and your private teacher review the recorded materials! Your teacher can provide insights you might miss. If it's really bad, make emergency plans to re-record. If you're happy with it, then get that recording delivered before the deadline.

December

Have Some Fun

With the pre-screenings recorded, now is the time to have some fun. Talk with your teacher and pick some fun pieces to play around with for a few weeks. I recommend my students put down the pieces that have occupied their time for so long and focus entirely on some fun, low-stress pieces.

Pause for the Holidays

High school is one of the few times in your life when you know you'll be around for the holidays. This part of life goes so quick that sometimes you just need to stop and smell the roses. Spend time with family and friends. When you practice, keep it light.

Wait Patiently

After months of preparing for your pre-screenings, it can be hard to stop thinking about them. Try anyway. Dwelling on things you can't change is a recipe for stress and anxiety. It'll wear you out emotionally without the benefit of impacting the results.

Just take comfort in the fact that you did your best and try to be patient.

January

Perform, Perform, Perform!

With the holidays over, it's time to gear up for audition season. Depending on where you apply, auditions could begin in the last week of this month, so you can't waste any time getting stage experience with your new pieces.

Take every opportunity that you can to perform the pieces you've been working on for so long. Going through the motions of a stage performance is the only thing that can begin to quell the nervousness that comes with performing live.

Instrument Inspection

You should have checked out your instrument before pre-screening, but now is another good time to address any required maintenance. It's particularly wise to get the green light from a luthier because *(depending on where you're auditioning)* your instrument is about to get exposed to a variety of climates. Make sure it can handle it.

Put Things on Replay

Play your pieces back to back. Auditions demand a ton of energy and focus. You need to guarantee that you can handle the entire length of your audition. If you invest the extra effort now, you can be sure that you have what it takes on the big day.

Personal Care

Musical performances are a physical activity and you should prepare for them the same way that an athlete prepares for a game. Ramp up your personal care by getting a full night's sleep every night, maintaining a healthy, balanced diet, and incorporating some exercise into your regular routine.

Wellness care promotes a healthy body and mind, two things you're going to want on audition day.

February

Plan Your Travel

February is a month of auditions, so you need to plan carefully. While you may want to save time and money by doubling up and cramming multiple auditions into a single day, it's a bad idea. You really need to take your time if you're going to do this right.

Are you able to fit in an extra day? If so, do it. Plan to use the extra time to visit the campus in a less formal way than you previously did.

Schedule Wisely

Whenever possible, plan to arrive in your audition city at least one night before you perform. That will help you get adjusted to any time zone or climate changes, in addition to giving you time to figure out practical issues, such as where to check-in and warm up.

Tips for a Perfect Audition

1. Take your time tuning. An audition isn't about speed. It's about precision.
2. Speak slowly and clearly. First impressions are important, so make sure that everything you say can be easily understood.
3. Pause between pieces. A moment between pieces allows faculty to collect their thoughts, process what they heard, and ask questions. It also helps you shift mentally to the next piece stylistically.

March

Reflect

At most, you have one or two auditions remaining. Give them everything you've got, and take a moment to reflect. You worked far harder than most college-bound students your age. You know what you want to do too, which is more than most of them can say.

Both of those are true achievements, so congratulations!

Start a Senior Recital Program

What — you thought that just because your auditions were over that you could take it easy? I don't think so!

Even as you wait to hear word about your auditions, you need to keep working. Young musicians that take lengthy breaks in their preparations end up lightyears behind their peers by the end of their careers. You need to keep working if you want to keep growing.

Schedule the Event

Figure out a date and venue for your recital. Be creative, if you want to be. You could invite other college-bound musicians to play with you, or present the recital as a fundraising opportunity to put you into a summer festival. It's up to you.

April

Evaluate

This is the moment you've all been waiting for. April is the month that your determination letters arrive. Hopefully your mailbox is stuffed with acceptances, but even if you get more rejections than you expected, you have a lot about which to be proud. You won't have much time to think about rejections, anyway, because you'll have a lot to consider.

Consult

Speak with your parents and your teacher to gauge their opinions and see how they can help you. They likely have insights you wouldn't consider, and may be able to shed some light on costs and repayment plans.

Consider all the factors. How much of an impact will your scholarship make? Are you impressed with the teacher? Was the campus agreeable to your needs?

Decide

After weighing all the options, make your decision. Take pride in all the work you put forth and the accomplishments you've made. Don't spend a minute second-guessing your decision. Just head right to the student store and buy a hoodie with the school's name on the front, because you're going to college!

CHAPTER 5

HOW TO BECOME AN ATTRACTIVE CANDIDATE FOR COLLEGES

If you've been paying attention so far, then you know how highly I value a musical education. If you want music to be a career, then you need to equip yourself with all the required skills and knowledge. That happens by going to college.

Across the board, college admissions are getting increasingly competitive. That means it can be harder to get accepted. In a sea of applicants, you want to stand out. If the admissions reps feel like you're a special student-musician, they will be more likely to accept you to their school. *(If you look hard, you may even find scholarships and grants to help you pay for tuition!)*

Some of my advice is obvious, but some of it is easy to overlook. When you're reading, think about how you would look to a stranger when compared to other students in each area. Any time that you think you could do better, create a plan to improve.

Score Good Grades

College is still school and one of the best ways to appear attractive to a college or university you want to attend is to demonstrate academic ability. A solid GPA is going to be one of the first things that an admissions rep will look for when they receive your application.

Certain schools require higher GPAs than others, but – obviously – they all want the highest GPAs possible, so study up.

<u>Testing Up & Out</u>

If you do well in school and can handle a challenge, then you may want to consider going above and beyond with some advanced placement *(AP)* classes. There are a variety of AP classes available *(including Music Theory)*. No matter your best subject, there is likely an AP class suited for your skills.

There are two reasons to take AP classes. The first is that they just look good to colleges. AP classes require extra dedication, a whole lot of hard work, and an additional test that evaluates your knowledge. All these requirements reflect well on a student, so colleges prefer students who take them.

The other reason goes beyond admissions.

AP tests are scored on a scale of 0-5, with five being the highest. If you score high enough, you may be able to "test out" of a required class in college. That is a huge win because it saves you time and money!

Even though most colleges won't let you test out of music classes, they may let you "test up" into an honors class that will be more challenging and teach you advanced skills and principles. Just be sure you know what you're getting into. All the extra time you pour into AP classes will take away from the time you can spend practicing your instrument.

Be Involved Musically

When it comes to your college application, only your musical ability and involvement is as important as your grades. That's because music programs don't accept talentless oafs with nothing more than a pipedream. They want musicians that have some level of talent already.

If you're using the 6 Pointers for Perfect Practice that I taught you in chapter 3, then I'm sure your skills are sufficient to get into a good school. That's why I'm going to talk about your musical involvement.

Getting Involved at School

Grades and talent are the two most important things that colleges look for in their applicants, but they get lots of smart and talented applicants like you. When that happens, they start looking at other factors, such as extracurricular involvement.

Extracurricular activities, such as school orchestra and pit band, are great additions to your résumé because they demonstrate:

- Your willingness to work hard
- A genuine enjoyment of music
- Basic social engagement
- Experience in a formal music setting
- Organizational and time management skills

Intangible factors like these make you look professional and mature. Those are the characteristics that schools want from their applicants.

Participating in Non-School Activities

School organizations are easy to join and can provide you with knowledge and experience, but they are not the only way to show an admissions rep how valuable you are. Participating in summer camps or performing locally as a volunteer can also be useful.

When you break the school activity barrier, it shows schools that you're not limited to standard options and that you can handle yourself in "real world" settings. As far as volunteer work is concerned, it also shows your compassion and personal interests. That's good because colleges are more than just academic institutions. They're also social ones, full of clubs, groups, and organizations that they want students to populate.

Perhaps just as important is that active, engaged students are the ones who are most beneficial to the school after graduation. They are more likely to donate after they graduate and are most likely to do exciting things, which reflects well on their alma mater.

Display Creativity and Motivation

You can really impress a school by stepping outside the box and using your talent in a fun and fascinating way. With technology and the internet, some really exciting options are available for you.

Unique Options for You

One of the ways that you can earn clients and increase your income down the road is to establish yourself as a leader in some portion of the music world. That's way easier to do if you get started now. Here are a few unique ways for you to set yourself apart from the competition as an applicant and as a professional:

- Organize an annual talent show
- Manage a marketing campaign for your school's arts programs
- Record a podcast and put it on iTunes
- Host a YouTube channel with original videos
- Start a classical music blog
- Write an industry newsletter
- Create your brand on social media
- Reach out to performers and develop strong relationships
- Write music-related Op-Eds for the local newspaper
- Form a chamber music ensemble
- Facilitate outdoor performances at fairs and other events

These and other creative pursuits will make you stand out from other people now and in the future. That makes you valuable.

Pursue Your Path

Not everyone knows the path that they want to pursue while they're in high school. If you know how you want to parlay your skills into a career after college, you're in a fortunate position because you can start laying your foundation today.

Here's why.

Suppose you know that you want to be an agent for strings musicians. What type of creative endeavor would benefit you the most? Obviously, it must be useful for agents.

For that reason, you may be better off interviewing local performance venues and publishing the interviews on a blog than you would be writing Op-Eds for the general public. That's because agents need professional contacts and an understanding of how venues hire. Op-Eds won't give you that, but a blog targeting string instrumentalists will answer the questions that they have and establish yourself as an intelligent would-be agent.

Be Smart on Social Media

Despite how fleeting it seems, most of what you do on the internet is permanent. It can be easily found, revealing your biggest victories as well as your biggest embarrassments. And that can be a problem.

More colleges than ever before are checking out the social media pages of their applicants. [1] I know it is fun liking and sharing and giving your opinions to friends and family, but social media can be dangerous if you don't use it properly. Famous and everyday people alike are taken down by stupid social media decisions all the time.

I'm not saying to delete all your social media channels, but it may be a good idea to make them private, especially if you like to say outlandish things or document your own questionable behaviors.

---

1 https://kidsprivacy.net/2016/01/20/more-college-admissions-using-social-media/

If you're not sure what constitutes questionable behavior, just consider whether you would be comfortable talking about it with your principal. If not, it should probably go.

Handle Your Business

Hoping to get their child into the best school, some parents take over the college application process. You cannot let that happen.

Involving your parents in your application process is something you can and should do. You can ask them questions or have them check for spelling errors. Even their insight could be valuable, but don't allow them to fill out your applications or manage your deadlines. I can tell you right now: no college wants a student who doesn't even fill out his or her own application.

That's why you need to find a way to seize back control from overreaching parents.

While your college applications should be mature, they don't need to be middle-aged adult mature. It's more important that they are an accurate reflection of you and your personality. An essay written by your mother won't do that – and your admissions rep will see right through it.

Julie Lythcott-Haims has seen lots of these overbearing parents. She "noticed a disturbing trend during her decade as a dean of freshmen at Stanford University. Incoming students were brilliant and accomplished and virtually flawless, on paper. But with each year, more of them seemed incapable of taking care of themselves." [2]

Does that sound like you? If so, it's not too late to change the script.

I'm no parenting expert, but I work with a lot of teenage musicians. I've got students who are entirely self-sufficient and I've got students who couldn't sign their own name without a parent's say-so. Those types of parents – you know, the ones who hover – are called helicopter parents.

Helicopter parents are around all the time and they're always trying to

2 https://www.washingtonpost.com/news/education/wp/2015/10/16/former-stanford-dean-explains-why-helicopter-parenting-is-ruining-a-generation-of-children/?utm_term=.dc197a45c3a8

make things easier for their kids. The problem is that they are almost never as helpful as they think they are. In fact, lots of times their involvement can be detrimental.

If you have helicopter parents, then you know that their efforts are well-intentioned. Still, it doesn't look good when a student seems incapable of handling their own business. Colleges want students, not student-parent teams. You must be independent.

Parents who hijack your application process probably think they are doing the right thing. They probably think they are doing you a favor. But they're not.

A note on helicopter parents: You're only in a position to rebut helicopter parents if you actually have everything under control. Parents can't be blamed for stepping in when you're letting deadlines fly by. Their instincts to help are just too strong.

Prepare for Your Prescreening

When I applied to schools for my undergrad, colleges hadn't yet begun requiring prescreening performances. I just submitted my applications and came in for an audition if they thought I looked good on paper.

When I went for my master's, schools all over the country were introducing prescreening performances to weed out unqualified applicants. Now everyone does it.

Prescreenings are video performances that you submit to schools with your application. Most schools will provide guidelines detailing exactly what they want to see from you. You'll probably need to upload your video to YouTube, although some schools may require the performance on DVD.

What People Don't Realize About Prescreening

Prescreening is as important as your audition

I'm not sure why students and parents don't seem to understand the significance of prescreening. Even though it goes by another name, prescreening is really your first round of auditions. If your prescreening performance doesn't make the cut, that's it. There's nothing else. It's game over before you even get your foot in the door.

You must give your prescreening the attention it deserves.

...but it's a little different

There's a balance to keep in mind when it comes to prescreenings. Of course, you want your performance to be as good as possible, but perfection isn't required.

Prescreenings are more of a glimpse into your ability then an outright examination. There are too many applicants to give all their prescreening videos full attention. Most of the time, your audience is only going to watch a minute or two at the beginning and the end, so don't stress about a missed note or two in the middle.

Quality recording is absolutely exhausting

Because playing our instruments is the fun part, it's easy to forget how tiring performance can be. When you record your prescreening performances, you're not going to walk in cold and nail each piece on the first try. I advise my students to plan for a long session. Usually, we're recording at least three takes of each piece.

If you're not used to playing your very best for very long, then that's something you'll need to work on. Build your stamina over time by incorporating pretend performances into your practice routine.

It takes a long time to prepare

Prescreening submissions are normally due on December 1st. If you're going to have a strong performance to showcase your skills, you need to begin preparing in the summertime.

Here are some of the things you'll need to do to prepare:

- Review each school's prescreening guidelines

- Consult with a parent or instructor on song selection
- Practice *(using my 6 Pointers for Perfect Practice)*
- Interview and hire a collaborative artist
- Identify your venue
- Hire a recording technician
- Build up your stamina

This process takes at least three months, from beginning to end. Wait too long and you'll regret it.

Make a Prescreening Video That Blows Away the Competition

Set up in a performance hall

The acoustics and visual appearance of a performance hall greatly improve the quality of your prescreening. This isn't the type of recording you want to make on the webcam in your living room. If you want to look and sound the part, you need to play in the right environment.

Wear formal attire

Similarly, you want to dress like a performer. For the gentlemen, a shirt, tie, pressed pants, and a nice pair of dress socks and shoes should do the trick. Ladies can also go the route of a shirt and slacks, but a conservative dress is the most common option.

Extra tip: If you have long hair, it's a good idea to wear it back, so your "audience" can see your face.

Hire help for the audio-visual recording

You're going to want to use professional recording equipment to film your prescreening, so the best thing to do is to hire someone who already has the equipment.

Even if you have quality gear and know how to use it, I really recommend hiring someone else. You're going to have a lot on your mind and it will be easier to focus on what you're doing if you have someone to handle the filming.

Don't waste time with introductions

I know that skipping the introduction feels impersonal, but the admissions department needs to move quickly. They'll have all the introduction that they'll need on your application. Just make sure to include a clear, descriptive title on the YouTube video and/or DVD.

Practice with your collaborative artist

The prescreening guidelines will usually require works with piano accompaniment. Once you find someone to work with, you'll want to practice with them. Iron out any wrinkles and make sure that you work well together. Like I said earlier, without a good prescreening performance, you'll never even get your foot in the door. Don't risk compromising your chances by using a collaborative artist that doesn't jive with you.

Keep Everything in Perspective

Although your experience in high school will help pave the way for your acceptance ino a good music school, it's important to be realistic. You're not a perfect musician. Mistakes happen.

A career is not defined by what happens in high school. It's not even defined by college, for that matter. These are stepping stones to the rest of your life. Treat them that way. I'm not suggesting that you disregard them entirely, but don't make mountains out of molehills. Practice hard. Stay humble. Stick to your routine. If you do these things, you're going to do well.

I guarantee it.

CHAPTER 6

SELECTING YOUR SCHOOL

If you follow the advice I've offered you in the preceding chapters, then you won't have to worry about being accepted into a music college. The only concern you'll have is deciding which school is best for you.

Going to a University vs. Going to a Conservatory

The biggest choice you'll make after committing to get a music education is deciding where you'll get it. One of the questions I get asked all the time concerns the difference between universities and conservatories.

Colleges & Universities

Colleges are schools that come after high school. Universities are groupings of schools that offer various degrees, including postgraduate options. They also require additional government accreditation. For the purposes of a music education, though, colleges and universities are basically the same.

Both offer a broad spectrum of classes that are available for you to take, even if they are outside of your music degree. Sometimes they are optional, but sometimes they are required. For instance, students of the University of Texas at Austin Butler School of Music are required to take a class called "The History of Texas," even though it's irrelevant to their degree.

Because they tend to be a little larger and have a wide range of classroom options, colleges and universities are the preferred destination of students who want to take out-of-curriculum classes like astronomy, statistics, or poetry.

Conservatory

Colleges and universities differ from conservatories primarily based on the grounds of focus and competition.

At a conservatory, you will be surrounded by people whose sole interest is in the arts. Your classes will be full of students who care only about music. Each of those classes will contribute directly towards furthering your knowledge and understanding of music.

A student majoring in Violin Performance may have a schedule like this:

- Music History
- Music Theory
- Secondary Piano
- Private Lessons
- Chamber Music
- Orchestra

(If you're lucky, you may have a class that I'd like to see in more universities: music business.)

You'll notice there is no English, chemistry, or political science on that roster. It's up to you to decide whether that's a good thing.

Another characteristic of conservatories is their competitiveness. Because they're so focused, great musicians want to teach and study there. This makes the application process hyper competitive. The competition remains even after acceptance, as students compete for the highest marks and best jobs after graduation.

Deciding Whether a University or Conservatory Is Best

Selecting where you would like to study after high school is obviously a matter of personal choice. What worked for me won't work for you.

The first thing to figure out is whether you want to attend a conservatory. Here are some questions to help guide you to the right answer:

- Would you prefer to take only classes that are relevant to your major?
- Are you comfortable bypassing a "well rounded" education in favor of something more specific?
- Are you 100% certain that you want to pursue a music career?

If you answered "yes" to those questions, you may be better suited for a conservatory than a college or university. Talk with your parents, teachers, and guidance counselor to get their input.

While every student has different interests, needs, and career paths, there are certain questions you can ask to help you decide which school is best for you. Keep reading to find some of the most important ones, as well as advice on how to find the answers.

Does the school have the correct focus?

You don't have to know exactly what you want to do to decide which specific school you want to attend. Sometimes, knowing a specific niche is enough.

That's because many schools specialize in a certain type of music or a particular performance style. For instance, the University of North Texas has one of the top jazz programs in the country. That school should be at the top of every jazz musician's list. Similarly, the Curtis Institute of Music is a premier school for violin.

How to know: A little bit of research should reveal which schools are a good fit for you and your specific goals. You can also check out what kind of performances a school produces. That's a good indicator of what their specialties are.

How good is its faculty?

When deciding on a school, there is no bigger concern than the quality of the faculty. That's because you go for the teacher, not for the school. Just as with prestigious math universities like MIT, music schools often attract students based on the appeal of their stellar faculty. That should be the draw for you too.

How to know: You should be in contact with professors at all the schools you apply to. Ask the questions that are most important to you and see how they respond. If their answers line up with your education goals, that's a good sign. Commentary about faculty online can also be illuminating.

Is it in the right location?

The best music schools tend to be right in the middle of the best music markets. One of the reasons that The Juilliard School is so terrific is that it is in a great location. It's within walking distance of Kaufman Music Center, Lincoln Center for the Performing Arts, and the Metropolitan Opera. If you don't think that's a symbiotic relationship, you're crazy.

The location of your college is likely to be the location of your young career, so there are other geographic concerns, too. Weather, cost of living, and patronage of the arts are just a few things you want to look for.

How to know: Bad access to good music, an impoverished population, and disinterest in the arts are all bad signs. You can learn whether your school checks the right boxes by visiting the campus and the surrounding area during your junior or senior year.

How much will it cost?

Depending on where you go to school, your college education could be one of the most expensive purchases you ever make. You want to make sure you don't spend that money foolishly.

This isn't something that many high school students are thinking about, but I would avoid accumulating debt whenever possible. It can really cripple you down the road. Selecting a slightly less prestigious school is a smart decision if it means you'll save tens of thousands of dollars.

How to know: Tuition costs are publicly posted on most schools' websites. A quick search should let you compare costs side-by-side.

A quick word on education finances

Long-term cost of student loans

Student loans provide access to an education that most students couldn't get otherwise. Still, they can be pricey. Federal loans usually come with an interest rate of about 6.8%. That's better than a credit card, but it's still $680 per year for every $10,000 you owe. After ten or fifteen years, it's a whole lot of money you're giving up.

Look for that scholarship money!

Scholarships can make expensive schools worthwhile and can make regular schools cheap! Whenever possible, you want to seek out scholarship money. Unless the school is a real dump, I think it's reasonable to attend a school primarily because they offer you a lot of money. *(That's how I chose Butler School of Music at The University of Texas at Austin for my master's degree!)*

Remember, selecting a school is a business decision. That means that cost plays an important role.

What do people say about it?

For better or worse, reputation matters when it comes to college. Going to a good school makes you more attractive to future clients and employers, even if you're only a mediocre talent.

Think about it this way: would you rather have a lawyer from Harvard or Wyoming State University? You'd probably prefer the one from Harvard. That's because Harvard's reputation is excellent. You have no idea if the Harvard grad was at the top of his class or the bottom. You don't know about his experience or his specialty. He could be a total loser compared to the WSU grad, but the Harvard graduate benefits from the school's reputation.

The same thing happens for music students.

How to know: Do a little research online or in industry magazines. Check out forums. Ask your teachers and instructors. Newspaper articles, ranking lists, and awards or recognitions can all reveal valuable information about reputation.

Are there good opportunities?

There's more to college than classrooms and textbooks. You also need the opportunity to practice what you learn and to perform with your instrument. As musicians, the opportunity to perform is especially important.

How to know: A school's own website should reveal how much opportunity a school offers its students. Schedules and event pages are particularly useful. Ask professors and people in your own network too.

Make a business decision

Although it's not the only factor that will determine your eventual success, selecting a college, university, or conservatory is a big deal. It will help set the trajectory for the rest of your career.

Decisions this big cannot be left to just the logical side or just the emotional side of your personality. The best choices will reflect both. You want to make sure that the program, the faculty, and the academics are of a high quality. You also want to make sure that the culture, the environment, and the intangibles are conducive to your emotional wellbeing. Without comfort, the technical stuff won't stick. Without musical excellence, happiness is just your mood.

The best school for you is the one at which both criteria complement each other. When that happens, you put yourself in a position to succeed, now and in the future.

CHAPTER 7

PUTTING WORDS INTO ACTION

I've come a long way since I played my first Itzhak Perlman album. I've gone through nine years of schooling, thousands of hours of practice, and countless emotional roller coasters. I haven't been able to figure it all out on the first try, but – in the end – I found my path.

You can do it too.

Using the advice I laid out in this book, you can transform the way you think about music, set yourself apart from your peers, milk high school for every ounce of opportunity, and get into a college that will offer you everything you need to succeed. This chapter contains a quick review of some of the most important concepts discussed in this book.

Remember That Music is a Business

In high school, music is a hobby. In college and beyond, it becomes a career.

The biggest challenge facing future professional musicians is the lack of business sense instilled in them at school. Few musicians know how to manage money, relationships, time, or other resources. From this moment forward, consider every aspect of your routine and each of your major decisions through the lens of business.

Is this behavior likely to help or hurt your business? What decisions can you make to protect what you've worked for and develop into a better musician? Music can still be fun, but it is also your livelihood. Treat it that way.

Find the Job for You

You're still young, but it's never too soon to begin narrowing down your career choices. Right off the bat, you may know what your ideal job looks like. If you don't, start giving it some thought.

Don't forget that there are lots of music jobs out there. You're not confined to the roles of performer or teacher. It's a big industry. You just need to find your place in it. *(At the end of this chapter is the appendix. In it, you'll find a list of 51 careers available to music majors. Check it out – I bet you'll find something you like.)*

Start Immediately

You might feel busy now, but high school truly is a quiet period in your life. As you get older, the responsibilities start pouring on and it gets harder and harder to dedicate time to your music. Every day that you fall behind now takes two days to catch up later.

That's why you need to begin working right now. Using the 8 Keys to Future Success from chapter 3, you can improve your technical, academic, social, and financial skills before you ever get to college. That kind of head start can put you years ahead of where you would be otherwise (not to mention years ahead of most of your peers). Remember: music is a business, and that means you need to have a whole bunch of skills. Practicing and playing well is only a single component. There's always something else to learn.

Stay on Track

As an adult, I can look back on my time in school and see that – as far as my career is concerned – school was just a series of checkpoints marking the path to where I wanted to go. The same is true for you.

Getting to your destination is much easier when you know the way. That's why I created the Strings Success Timetable. In it, I lay out all the major high school checkpoints for you. Use it carefully and you'll be on track throughout your entire high school career.

Preserve Your Reputation

While you shouldn't waste your life worrying about what other people think, the reality of business is that reputations do matter. You should pay attention to all the high-visibility criteria that influence your standing in the industry.

As a student, that means studying hard and scoring a strong GPA. It means getting musically involved in extracurricular activities, volunteer performances, and paid events. It means keeping questionable material off your Snapchat and other social media profiles.

You must remain aware of how your behavior impacts your opportunities. What you do today can affect how schools, partners, and future employers view you tomorrow.

Select Your Perfect School

The knowledge and technical skill you pick up at school will form the foundation of your career. Without that education, it is difficult to develop into the professional you want to be.

Still, I don't want you to become a nervous wreck trying to get into the best school. Certain colleges, universities, and conservatories may have a better staff than others. They may have more resources or better opportunities, too. In the end, however, school is merely a means to an end.

You can go to a top-ten music school and never earn a nickel. You can go to an off-the-radar college in a small town and end up selling out arenas. That's why you need to focus on getting into the perfect school for you. Remember to consider all the factors.

- Is a college/university or a conservatory better for you?
- Do your top schools focus on your specialties and/or career paths?
- Does the distance from home play a role in your decision?
- How does the teacher suit your personality? Will you be a good fit together?
- What type of opportunities will you have?
- Is the price right?

These factors – and others, discussed in Chapter 6 – will help you determine which schools are best for you and your professional goals.

Never Stop Working

Careers in the music industry are rarely like other careers. You'll find that there usually isn't a clear path to get you where you want to go. That's up to you. Teachers, friends, and books like this one can help give you direction, but success requires individual characteristics. Specifically, it requires discipline, business sense, and – most of all – hard work.

As a high school student, you'll run into tough teachers, awkward social situations, difficult decisions, and new musical challenges. Keep working.

As a college student, you'll have to embrace a new place, new friends, new musical skills, and an overwhelming blank slate to carve out the rest of your career. Keep working.

In your career, you'll face money problems, constant doubt, a new level of expectation, and the challenge of finding new ways to grow. Keep working.

If you love music as much as I do, then you have all the motivation you could ever need to find success. Every challenge can be conquered. Every goal can be achieved. Success requires relentless focus and attention, but I know you can do it. There are no problems that you can't work out.

APPENDIX

RESOURCES AND EXAMPLES

Bonus #1: My Killer Career List - 51 Music Careers for Music Majors

If you didn't see anything interesting among the six music careers I listed back in chapter 3, don't worry. There are plenty more music jobs available for smart and talented musicians. Here are 51 for you to start thinking about.

I've made the decision to include approximate salary figures here, but don't treat them as guarantees. Salaries depend on ability and need, vary by region, and go up and down over time. All the salaries listed will give you a pretty good idea of what to expect for a particular career, but your experience may vary.

MUSIC THERAPIST

What they do: Use the power of music to help individuals attain peace and health. Music therapy is common in institutions, such as schools, rehabs, prisons, and nursing homes. Some music therapists work as solo entrepreneurs, maintaining a freelance relationship with referring professionals.

Perks: Help people get healthy.
Earnings: Established music therapists earn around $50k/year.
Perfect for: People who want to help others.

PRIVATE INSTRUCTOR

What they do: Educate aspiring musicians of all talent levels on the use of a specific instrument, including the voice. Most instructors teach middle and high school students. Even some young professionals maintain private instructors for a little while.

Perks: Set your own hours. Deep satisfaction.
Earnings: $25k/year to start; up to $150k/year for advanced instructors in good markets.
Perfect for: Observant, goal-oriented people who can see the long-term.

COLLABORATIVE ARTIST

What they do: Collaborative artists, or accompanists, work primarily with solo performers to provide backup vocals or instrumentation.

Perks: Knowing a vast amount of repertoire and exposure to potential clients.
Earnings: Hourly. Normally in the range of $25-70/hour *(though your negotiating skills could be a factor here).*
Perfect for: Performers comfortable with collaboration.

COLLEGE EDUCATOR (NOT K-12)

What they do: College educators teach students like you. They work with music students at colleges, universities, and conservatories.

Perks: Meet hundreds *(or thousands)* of young musicians. Earn credibility.

Earnings: There are many types of college educators and they all earn different wages. Lecturers can earn as little as $25k/year, while top professors can earn six figures.

Perfect for: Musicians who love to learn and explain what they've learned.

PERFORMANCE AGENT

What they do: Agents book one-time and ongoing jobs for their clients, who are performers. They build networks of contacts to ensure that their clients have frequent, fair-paying work.

Perks: You get to pull back the curtain on the negotiating/contact-building side of things *(which is great if you ever decide that you want to perform yourself)*.

Earnings: Generally commission-based. Many agents pull in 15% of what they negotiate for their clients.

Perfect for: Good communicators with business sense who are unafraid of professional negotiation.

INDEPENDENT APP DEVELOPER

What they do: Create mobile device software for musicians. Examples would be apps that help you tune an instrument or identify a composition. Obviously, the sky *(or your creativity)* is the limit with this one.

Perks: Lets you work from home and gives you a business reason to buy the new tech toys you already wanted.

Earnings: Highly dependent on the success of your apps. *(Work for a*

company, though, and you could make $80k/year.)
Perfect for: A tech-savvy musician who likes to solve problems.

MUSIC WEBSITE SPECIALIST

What they do: Design and build websites for artists, ensembles, and organizations. Use an intimate understanding of the web and the music industry to create compelling websites musicians can use as their go-to place online. Mostly freelance, though some work in design agencies.

Perks: Creative expression and intimate access to artists.
Earnings: $500-$10,000/website, depending on difficulty.
Perfect for: Artistic people with technological skills.

ARRANGER

What they do: Arrangers take existing music and re-conceptualize it for a new purpose. They might tinker with the harmony of a composer's piece, or orchestrate his or her score for a new instrument.

Perks: Work with talented people and develop highly useful skills.
Earnings: $20-$40k/year is normal.
Perfect for: People interested in the theory and manipulation of music.

AUDIO ENGINEER

What they do: Technician who records and mixes audio for future production. Basic challenges may require specific manipulations to cancel out feedback or background noise.

Perks: Work with performers and *(occasionally)* have creative input regarding the final product.
Earnings: Somewhere around $45k/year is normal.
Perfect for: A fan of the modern recording and production process.

BLOG WRITER

What they do: Bloggers create written content for consumption online. They could take a journalistic approach and cover music news and trends, or they could take a more casual approach and write opinion-based pieces.

Perks: Work remotely and have an outlet for your voice and opinions.
Earnings: Almost always starts as an unpaid hobby, but get enough readers and you can make six figures per year.
Perfect for: A motivated individual with writing and (possibly) research skills.

BUSINESS MANAGER

What they do: Business managers keep music businesses from going under by overseeing financial, organizational, and resource-related problems. Examples of music businesses could include theatres, record stores, agencies, or just about anything else.

Perks: Control the "big picture" for a business or organization.
Earnings: Depending on the size and success of the business you manage, anywhere from $40k/year to $175k/year is possible.
Perfect for: Organized people who can successfully oversee multiple projects at the same time.

CHAMBER MUSICIAN

What they do: Perform in an ensemble with other musicians. Ensembles nowadays play anywhere from traditional concert halls to local "club" venues. Many perform at weddings and similar one-off events.

Perks: You get to perform, and maybe even manage the group (if you started your own ensemble).
Earnings: Depends on countless factors. A full-time chamber musician could make $10k/year or $100k/year.
Perfect for: A performer.

CONCERT COMPOSER

What they do: Writes scores intended for performance, and not for use in films or other projects. Most concert composers write classical or contemporary music.

Perks: Creative freedom.
Earnings: Hard to give an accurate number because most composers begin writing "on the side" before developing into a full-time career.
Perfect for: People primarily interested in writing music.

PROMOTER

What they do: May work solo or with a company to promote a performance or series of performances. Usually, a promoter works with a venue, not a specific group or artist.

Perks: You get to attend many performances.
Earnings: Promoter contracts can be salary or commission-based. $50k/year is reasonable, though the world's top promoters can make seven figures.
Perfect for: Those who see the value in other artists and can persuade other people to see it also.

ADMINISTRATION

What they do: Works for a large professional organization, such as an opera house or college. Duties vary, but involve logistical work, like writing grants, processing payroll, and maintaining schedules.

Perks: Work with big-budget employers.
Earnings: Start at normal entry-level salary *($30-$50k/year)* with room for advancement.
Perfect for: Detail-oriented people who don't need to be near the stage.

CONDUCTOR

What they do: Provide instructive gestures concerning tempo and interpretation to performers in an orchestra.

Perks: Enjoy intimate proximity to the music and get a lot of attention.
Earnings: Most conductors do not work for major orchestras, and so earn something equivalent to a professor's salary from their school or institution. The "big guys" can make $500k/year.
Perfect for: Technical masters with a knowledge of many instruments.

CRUISE PERFORMER

What they do: Perform for audiences on board luxury cruise ships. Most cruise ships offer seasonal contracts for performers.

Perks: See beautiful places and *(sometimes)* enjoy free meals/ entertainment.
Earnings: Salaried according to budget and talent. Something in the range of $500-$1800 weekly is reasonable.
Perfect for: Single performers who don't mind living where they work.

SCORE ENGRAVER

What they do: Transcribe the handwritten score of a composer so that it can be reproduced and distributed. Normally, a professional notation program such as Sibelius is used.

Perks: Work closely with composers and see new music first.
Earnings: Most of the work is for freelance engravers, but you can earn up to $50,000 per year if you're working full-time.
Perfect for: Those who are detailed and organized.

DIRECTOR OF ENSEMBLE

What they do: Organizes and/or manages a new musical ensemble (or takes over an existing one). They may conduct, but are always in charge of scheduling, finances, and rehearsals.

Perks: Directors get to implement their musical voice.
Earnings: As much as you can convince someone to pay you, in the beginning. If you're able to work your way up to directing orchestras, you could make millions.
Perfect for: Passionate creative types with another income stream or two.

MUSIC EVENT PLANNER

What they do: Just like any other kind of event planners, they handle the planning, logistics, talent acquisition, and marketing of a scheduled event. Examples include competitions, fundraisers, festivals, and weddings.

Perks: Planners get to hand-pick the talent at their events.
Earnings: Someone putting in full time hours can pull $35k-$45k/year.
Perfect for: You, if you're organized and love planning parties.

FILM & TV COMPOSER

What they do: Write music for movies, documentaries, and television shows.

Perks: Enjoy the satisfaction of hearing your work used in popular culture.
Earnings: The average earnings depend on what medium you're writing for. TV shows run $4k-$10k per episode. Studios may pay tens of thousands for the music of a popular film. Film composers like John Williams can command millions.
Perfect for: Composers who are comfortable writing for someone else's vision.

FILM & TV CONDUCTOR

What they do: Direct the musicians who are recording the score for a film or TV show.

Perks: Regular immersion in new music.
Earnings: Depends on the size of the studio and its budget. American Federation of Music guidelines usually require the conductor to be paid twice what is paid to the performers.
Perfect for: Conductors who don't need the recognition of the orchestral conductor.

MUSICOLOGIST

What they do: Study music from different cultures and times in history. Nearly all musicology work is academic, so most musicologists work at universities or museums. Frequently, they write or teach about their findings.

Perks: Freedom to explore music of all types.
Earnings: About the same as a college professor.
Perfect for: Music eggheads.

COMMERCIAL COMPOSER

What they do: Create hooks and jingles for advertisements or music banks. Most work as independent contractors, but a few work with agencies. The best can write tunes that become synonymous with the brand they're advertising. *(I'm sure you can think of one right now...)*

Perks: Some measure of creative freedom and control over your own schedule.
Earnings: Payments are earned on a per-jingle basis. Big companies will pay up to $8,000 for a single tune if it's for a large campaign.
Perfect for: Creative types who don't need a spotlight.

FOLEY ARTIST

What they do: Create the non-musical "soundtrack" to scenes being filmed for movies or television. Normally, their work consists of everyday sounds like blowing wind, crunching glass, etc. Often freelance.

Perks: Access to, and involvement in, film industry.
Earnings: Between $200-$400/day, depending on skill and union membership.
Perfect for: Creative people who like solving problems.

DEVELOPMENT ASSISTANT

What they do: Work with a non-profit organization to solicit donations. Primary responsibilities include organizing fundraisers, calling donors, writing grants, and tracking goal progress. Sometimes freelance.

Perks: You get to be a part of something important.
Earnings: Full-time development assistants earn around $50k/year on average.
Perfect for: Organized, outgoing personalities not intimidated by money talk.

INSTRUMENTAL CRAFTSMAN

What they do: Build new or maintain existing musical instruments. Can work entirely independently, if desired.

Perks: Free or discounted instruments.
Earnings: Livable salaries if you work with a company, but can make $150,000+/year if you make it big as a custom builder.
Perfect for: Musicians who are good with their hands.

MUSICAL PRODUCT DEMONSTRATOR

What they do: Plays instruments to demonstrate their features and quality. Demonstrates non-instrumental products. Sometimes freelance.

Perks: Get to see the newest toys.
Earnings: Standard marketing salaries. $60k-$100k/year.
Perfect for: Musicians who can play a little bit of everything and have a knack for selling.

MUSIC STORE SALESPERSON

What they do: Salespeople sell instruments, accessories, and other equipment. Usually, they sell to individuals in a brick and mortar shop.

Perks: Low-stress work. Discounts.
Earnings: Usually around $45k/year.
Perfect for: Chatty people who are knowledgeable about instruments and gear.

PRODUCTION SOUND MIXER

What they do: Production Sound Mixers capture all the sound created on-set during movie or television filming. This includes actor dialogue. Also known as Location Sound Engineers. Sometimes freelance.

Perks: High quality equipment and industry access.
Earnings: Average salaries are about $53k/year.
Perfect for: People who understand how to use mics and mixers well.

SONGWRITER

What they do: Write music and/or lyrics. Some songwriters turn around and perform their creations. Others sell them to third parties. Mostly freelance.

Perks: Creative outlet. Get to hear your work performed.
Earnings: Vary widely. Earnings opportunities come from ticket sales, licensing agreements, royalties, and so on.
Perfect for: Composers and lyricists.

"FRONT OF HOUSE" ENGINEER

What they do: Operate the mixer during live musical *(or theatre)* productions. If a venue has a sound team, the FOH engineer will manage them as well.

Perks: Be a part of frequent live shows.
Earnings: $35k-$90k/year.
Perfect for: Graduates with technical knowledge who can solve problems quickly.

MARKETER

What they do: Promote products, services, events, people, and ideas. Digital marketing, which uses social media and the internet, is a particularly popular avenue these days.

Perks: Work remotely. Creative freedom.
Earnings: Entry level marketers earn as little as $10/hour, but big-timers can earn $80k/year.
Perfect for: People who are persuasive and confident.

MASTERING ENGINEER

What they do: Mastering engineers deal with the final mix of an audio recording. They usually enhance the mix and save it to its final storage device. Most are freelance.

Perks: Work with sophisticated technology.
Earnings: Freelance mastering engineers earn on a per-track or per-album basis. $150-$300/track is reasonable.
Perfect for: Techies with a good ear.

DIRECTOR OF THE CHOIR

What they do: Choir directors manage all aspects of the choir, such as auditions, rehearsals, budget planning, and scheduling and conducting performances.

Perks: Wield managerial and creative control.
Earnings: $20k-$50k/year is reasonable for a church's director, but others may pay differently.
Perfect for: An organized and skilled vocalist.

MILITARY PERFORMER

What they do: The U.S. has a rich history with military ensembles. All the major branches of military have multiple bands and ensembles *(except the Coast Guard, which has just one)*. Military performers play in the band for graduations, commissioning of equipment, and parades.

Perks: Play music while serving your country. Partial tax exemptions on
salary.
Earnings: If accepted into premier groups, immediately receive E6 rank. Plus, earn about $50k/year, with housing and meal allowances.
Perfect for: Musicians with a serious sense of patriotism.

MUSIC THEATER PERFORMER

What they do: Act in stage productions. Music theater separates itself from regular theater productions because there is singing and dancing, in addition to acting. Sometimes freelance.

Perks: Live performances and stage time.
Earnings: About $500/week, unless you work on Broadway. Broadway productions pay performers closer to $1800/week.
Perfect for: Singing specialists with a flair for drama.

MUSIC CURATOR

What they do: Curators manage and present music collections. Usually, they'll work with colleges, large libraries, or museums to preserve and play historic collections.

Perks: Get to work hands-on with old collections.
Earnings: Start at $50,000/year, with large institutions.
Perfect for: Fans of music history.

EDUCATION ADMINISTRATOR

What they do: Hire and fire staff, facilitate operations, and alter curriculum. Administrators work in elementary, middle, and high schools, as well as at the university level.

Perks: Implement education ideas.
Earnings: Depends on a lot of factors. $20k-$80k/year is normal.
Perfect for: Organized and education-minded people who don't want to teach.

ATTORNEY

What they do: Just like every product needs a salesman, every artist needs an attorney. Music and entertainment attorneys represent artists and organizations in contract disputes, lawsuits, copyright infringement cases, and many other legal matters.

Perks: Close involvement in two very different fields.
Earnings: Attorney earnings depend on their clients. Represent a few low-level artists and you could struggle to pay the rent. Work for a major
entertainment firm and you could make $160k+ in your first year!
Perfect for: Law-minded music lovers.

CRITIC, OR MUSIC JOURNALIST

What they do: Critics mostly write reviews about albums, live performances, events, and artists. Sometimes they write books or participate in panel discussions. Music journalists stick to newsworthy stories about trends, events, and the industry at large. Sometimes freelance.

Perks: Listen to, and attend, performances frequently.
Earnings: Depends on which outlet publishes your work. $25k-$75k/year is definitely reasonable for a talented writer.
Perfect for: Observant and persuasive writers.

MUSIC SUPERVISOR

What they do: Make the music-related decisions for a specific project. Music supervisors can work on movies, TV shows, commercials, video games, and documentaries.

Perks: Get to implement creative vision.
Earnings: Start at about $30k/year.
Perfect for: Confident decision-makers who can see "the big picture."

ORCHESTRAL MUSICIAN

What they do: I probably don't need to explain this one. Orchestral musicians play their instrument as part of a symphony orchestra.

Perks: Live the fantasy. Perform regularly.
Earnings: There are large and small markets all over the country with vastly different pay scales. The Victoria Symphony pays a per-service fee of approximately $100 per rehearsal or performance. The New York Philharmonic pays about $136,000 annually.
Perfect for: Musicians who can't shake the desire to perform in an orchestra.

INSTRUMENT TUNER

What they do: Instrument tuners restore the ideal sound to an instrument by tuning it properly. Piano tuning is the best opportunity to make some money unless you're tuning instruments for a small orchestra. Mostly freelance.

Perks: Good side gig.
Earnings: Up to $200 per piano tuning.
Perfect for: Pianists with a main income stream.

SALES REP FOR PUBLISHER

What they do: Sell completed compositions to individual artists and record labels. Sometimes referred to as "pluggers."

Perks: See new compositions first.
Earnings: $30k-$60k/year.
Perfect for: Persuasive people who can manage large networks.

RADIO DISC JOCKEY (DJ)

What they do: Entertain listeners with banter, personality, and – of course – music. Part of a DJ's role is to present a personality that matches the character of the radio station.

Perks: Notoriety without performing.
Earnings: About $50k/year, for popular radio stations.
Perfect for: Bold and interesting personalities.

SESSION ARTIST

What they do: Play on recording projects, normally as the second or third instrument. Could work with any artist who needs another musician to record with. Frequently freelance.

Perks: Work with a variety of artists and labels.
Earnings: Many session artists are paid $200-$500 per session. Gain credibility and you can push that number into the thousands.
Perfect for: Performers who don't need to take the lead.

TOUR MANAGER

What they do: Organizes an artist's performance tour. Tour managers book hotels, plan transportation, make reservations, facilitate promotional events, and handle all kinds of other logistics.

Perks: Form personal relationships with artists.
Earnings: The bigger the artist, the more you make. Good managers make $80k+/year.
Perfect for: Highly organized people who handle stress easily.

ORCHESTRATOR

What they do: Takes an existing score and arranges it into something suitable for a larger ensemble, or even an entire orchestra.

Perks: Get to interpret *(or reinterpret)* existing compositions.
Earnings: Normally between $40-$80 for every four measures of music.
Perfect for: Composers willing to work with someone else's vision.

ARTS & REPERTOIRE (A&R) REP

What they do: A&R reps work with record label companies to scout talent. Pop culture has taught us that talent scouts focus on more mainstream genres, but there are labels of all kinds, and they all need talented artists.

Perks: Watch lots of performances and pow-wow with talented up-and-coming artists.
Earnings: $25k/year to start; up to $80k/year for talented reps with a proven record.
Perfect for: Observant, social people with analytical skills.

Bonus #2: Some Notes about Instrument Maintenance

Instruments are unlike any other purchase that you make. They start off expensive and get more expensive over time. The most famous violins of all, those made by the Italian families called Stradivari and Guarneri, were crafted in the late 17th and 18th centuries. Today, pristine models can pull millions of dollars at auction. *(The highest ever purchased cost the buyer $15.9 million!)*

While your instrument is unlikely to fetch a price that high in your lifetime, they can still be costly. Even college musicians often own instruments worth over $10,000. With price tags like that, the importance of proper instrument maintenance is obvious. As much as stocks or index funds, a good string instrument is an investment.

Here's how to protect it.

STRINGS

The strings are clearly a vital part of your instrument, and play an essential role in your ability to practice and perform. Most of my life I never gave much attention to the strings. I just played them forever, until they broke or started giving me trouble. That changed recently.

Not too long ago, I spoke at a small conference with one of the top officers at Thomastik. Naturally, we got to discussing strings.

He told me that life of a string is well established. Just like a car that needs regular oil changes to run at its best, string instruments need a steady diet of new strings. Although it may last longer, you can expect a string to perform at its best for only 300 hours. After that, it's time to swap. If you press on any longer, wear and tear causes your sound quality to suffer.

So, here's the obvious question: how do you know when you've played

300 hours? Luckily, I've already recommended the perfect solution for this problem. All you need to do is keep a running tally of total play time in your practice journal.

(For what it's worth, I also like to keep a spare set of strings around, in case the 300-hour mark sneaks up on me, or I damage a string somehow.)

BOWS

Your bow is nearly as important as the instrument itself. To keep both at tip-top shape, you must plan for regular bow rehairing. As you probably suspected, your bow won't last forever. Just like your strings, the hair on a bow suffers from wear and tear, sacrificing its ability to create beautiful tone.

To keep it performing optimally, you may want to have a rehair at least twice annually.

Another thing you must do to ensure that your bow performs optimally is to use rosin. Rosin serves the purpose of increasing hair friction on the strings, which allows the strings to "speak" more clearly. You should rosin your bow every day.

FINGERBOARDS

Did you know that dropping your fingers on the fingerboard can create grooves? Fingerboard grooves reduce its smoothness and impact intonation. If your fingers are falling into the grooves on your instrument's fingerboard, your intonation is probably suffering.

You should visit a specialist and find out whether a little TLC is required.

BRIDGE

Your instrument is made of wood, and wood is seriously affected by the weather. Introducing your instrument to changing climate can warp the bridge. Extreme temperatures can even cause the body of the violin to split or crack. This is one of the reasons why you never want to leave your instrument in your vehicle. *(The other reason is that it could be a temptation to would-be thieves.)*

Warping isn't the exclusive result of weather. Changing the strings is also enough to affect the bridge. I've even known a violin's bridge to shift out of place because it was too loose in its case. The bouncing was enough to jolt the bridge out of place.

All these issues are problematic because when the bridge is out of place, it changes the angle at which the bow touches the strings. That changes the sound.

SOUND POST

Another victim of changing climates is your instrument's sound post. The sound post is responsible for much of an instrument's character. Its location can cause the sound to be dark or bright, warm or hard, powerful or weak.

If you think your instrument is undergoing a change, or that it just doesn't sound quite how you want it to, the sound post may be to blame. A luthier can adjust your sound post to target the characteristics that you want. Ignoring the sound post can allow your instrument to fall further and further from the sound you like.

Bonus #3: Fill-in-the-Blank Email Template for Contacting Professors

Every time you meet a professor for the first time you must treat it like an audition. Be as prepared as you possibly can. One way to prepare is to compile a list of questions about the school, teaching staff, and programs. Some good questions include:

- Will I be receiving a lesson every week?

- How many people are in your studio?

- What is the ratio between undergraduate, graduate and doctoral students?

- How many openings do you have for the upcoming year?

- Are you planning on going on a Sabbatical sometime in the near future?

(I never used to encourage students to ask about staff sabbaticals, but several of my students have encountered it.)

When the time comes to meet your future professor(s), make sure you take your most polished pieces. Why? Because you need to treat your first meeting like an audition – remember? If you are seriously interested in that teacher or school, try to go to the school and visit the professor before the week of your audition. Nothing shows interest more than taking the time to plan an early visit.

The best time to e-mail a teacher about setting up a pre-audition lesson is at the end of the summer. Most professors are teaching, performing, and vacationing during the summer, so it is very difficult to meet a professor during that time.

Of course, you can avoid this communication drought altogether by attending a festival that features your preferred professor. If you know who you want to study with, then this is my best advice. Invest the money, time, and energy, go directly to where your future mentor is!

Getting one lesson with a potential teacher before you go study with them is great, but more is better. If you have the opportunity to receive multiple lessons, you can really see how they would work with you. That is ideal. Remember that this is an investment. The next four *(or two or three)* years of your life depend on what kind of relationship you have with your professor. Compared to a college education, the upfront cost of a festival is tiny. Pay for the festival and you can make a smarter long-term investment when it comes to college *(and professor)* selection.

Whether or not you can attend a festival where your preferred professor is, you want to remember the fact that your initial contact is a type of audition, no matter whether it's face-to-face or by e-mail. First impressions are everything. Many professors will make up in their minds about whether you're worth meeting just by reading your e-mail.

With that in mind, you want make sure that your first e-mail to a future professor looks great. Mess this one up and you could shoot yourself in the foot. Turn the page to see how I would write the e-mail. Feel free to use it yourself. Just fill in the blanks and you've got a credible letter to your future professor!

Dear Professor _____,

My name is _____ and I am currently a senior at _____ studying with _____. My teacher has said wonderful things about your teaching and thinks that you may be a very good fit for me and has therefore encouraged me to apply for your studio. I would love the opportunity to come and visit the school and to possibly receive a trial lesson from you at your convenience. I understand that your schedule is very busy, so if you have a few possible dates or times that might work well with your availability, I would be so appreciative if you could share them with me. Thank you so much for your time and consideration, and I look forward to hearing from you.

Sincerely,

_____

Bonus #4: Résumé Template
(and A Completed Example!)

Résumés are the summary of all your experience. They're used to introduce you to potential employers, festivals, and other programs. On the next page, you'll see a template that you can use to create your very own résumé. Keep in mind that every résumé should be tailored to display your credentials for the specific position you're applying for.

Some people love the one-page rule for résumés. I'm comfortable with a two-pager, but much longer than that is usually a pretty bad idea. Remember: the reader likely has a stack of résumés from a bunch of qualified candidates. If yours is too long, they'll probably just move on to the next one.

Formatting is also important. Your résumé should look like an organized document that gives the highlights of your career. It should not read like a book report.

For example:

Full Name
Address
Email address | Phone number

<u>Work Experience</u>

[Start date] – [Finish date]: [Role or job title #1]

Here you want to type a few short sentences describing what you did. For jobs, explain your responsibilities – especially those responsibilities that relate to the new job you want. For performances, include any relevant details. You may have several "Experience entries." List them in reverse chronological order, and don't feel the need to list the really old stuff.

[Start date] – [Finish date]: [Role or job title]

Extra formatting, such as boldface, italicization, or underlining, can help make your résumé easy to read. That's important because you want readers to be able to skim it quickly. Another quick-skim trick that I love is to use bullet points. Bullet points are great because they:

- Summarize information quickly

- Break up the monotony of boring paragraphs

- Draw attention to important points

Performance Experience

- [Your Role] – [Type of Performance], [Group Performed With]

- Permanent Member – Soloist, Hometown Orchestra

Education

The older you get, the more information you may be able to put here. As a young musician, your school and studio are sufficient. As a college graduate, you can enter your school this way:

- [Year of Graduation]: [Name of your Degree]; [Your College's Name]

- 2020: Bachelor's of Sample Entry; The University of Examples

References

Even as a middle or high school student, you have references. Include your private instructor and/or teachers. Anybody who can speak about your personality and/or skill is appropriate. It's generally a good idea to let them know you're using them, though.

- [Reference's Name]: [Title], [Employer or Institution] | [Contact info]

- Mr. Jimmy James: Private Instructor, James' Music Institute | jjames@example.com

Pasha Sabouri
123 Main Street | Austin, TX 78701
pashasabouri@gmail.com | 512.555.5555

Teaching Experience

January 2015 – January 2016: Assistant Orchestra Director St. Andrew's Episcopal Upper School.

2014 - Present: Founder and Artistic Director of Texas Strings Camp.

A non-profit organization that hosts world-class musicians from around the World in Austin, providing advanced instruction for talented young string musicians. More information can be found at TexasStringsCamp.com

August 2013 – Present: Hired as Consultant for Akins, Lake Travis, Westlake Orchestra, Bedichek Orchestras.

Job Duties Included:

- Writing bowings and fingerings in all parts for each section
- Giving sectionals
- Clinicing the full orchestra for UIL preparation

August 2013 – January 2015: Adjunct Professor of Strings at University of Mary Hardin Baylor

- Teach both major and non-majors in violin
- Lead and conduct the College Chamber Orchestra
- Teach music pedagogy courses (String Methods)

August 2010 – August 2013: Adjunct Professor of Strings at Concordia University

- Recruited first violin major to the university

- Teach both major and non-majors in violin
- Lead and conduct the Concordia Chamber Orchestra
- Teach music elective classes *(Introduction to World Music, Conducting)*

August 2010 – August 2012: Violin Instructor - Akins High School

- Teach violin lessons - 98% of students eligible for free lunch program
- Lead sectionals for the orchestra and the violin sections

August 2009 – August 2010: Guest Lecturer – Centenary College (Shreveport, LA)

- Conduct the advanced pre-college orchestra
- Coached top 4 all-state chairs, 5 winners of school concerto competition, and grand prize winner to perform on Shreveport Radio
- Refined technique, recital preparation, and Louisiana competitions
- Teach individual lessons to 16 pre-college students and 6 college majors
- Teach group Suzuki classes for books 1, 2, and 3

August 2006 - August 2009: Teaching Assistant to Brian Lewis - The University of Texas at Austin

- Teach individual scales and technique lessons to Brian Lewis's undergraduate violin studio
- Teach 16 hours each week, including majors and non-majors
- Teach individual violin lessons to non-majors
- Lead group performances of I Soloisti Verdiani

Performing Experience

- Substitute – Minnesota Orchestra
- Permanent Member – River Oaks Chamber Orchestra (Houston)
- Played with Austin Symphony, Austin Lyric Opera, Las Vegas Philharmonic
- Soloed with Las Vegas Philharmonic, Balcones Community Orchestra, Ottawa Chamber Orchestra, Henderson Symphony

Education

- 2010: Doctor of Musical Arts; The Butler School of Music at the University of Texas at Austin

- 2007: Master of Music; The Butler School of Music at the University of Texas at Austin
- 2004: Bachelors of Music; The University of Cincinnati College Conservatory of Music

References

- Brian Lewis: Professor of Violin, The University of Texas at Austin
512.555.5555 | email@emailcom

- Jinjoo Cho: Professor of Violin, Oberlin Conservatory and Cleveland Institute of Music
512.555.5555 | email@emailcom

- Naoko Tanaka: Professor of Violin, The Juilliard School
512.555.5555 | email@emailcom